GREENE'S GROATSWORTH OF WIT

Bought with a Million of Repentance

(1592)

Attributed to

Henry Chettle and Robert Greene

CDEDIEVAL & RENAISSANCE

TEXTS & STUDIES

VOLUME 114

GREENE'S
GROATSWORTH
OF WIT

Bought with a Million of Repentance

(1592)

Attributed to

Henry Chettle and Robert Greene

Edited by

D. Allen Carroll

Binghamton, New York

1994

Library of Congress Cataloging-in-Publication data

Chettle, Henry, d. 1607?
    Greene's Groatsworth of wit : bought with a million of repentance
(1592) / attributed to Henry Chettle and Robert Greene ; edited by D.
Allen Carroll.
       p. cm. —(Medieval & Renaissance texts & studies ; v. 114)
    ISBN 0–86698–167–5
    1. Greene, Robert, 1558?–1592—Biography. 2. Authors, English—
Early modern, 1500–1700—Biography. 3. Shakespeare, William, 1564–
1616. I. Greene, Robert, 1558?–1592. II. Carroll, D. Allen (Daniel
Allen), 1938– . III. Title. IV. Title: Groatsworth of wit. V. Series.
PR2280.G44Z62 1993
828'.309—dc20   93–6276
                                                                    CIP

This book is made to last.
It is set in Plantin, smythe-sewn
and printed on acid-free paper
to library specifications

Printed in the United States of America

GREENES,

GROATS-VVORTH
of witte, bought with a
million of Repentance.

Deſcribing the follie of youth, the falſhood of make-
ſhifte flatterers, the miſerie of the negligent,
and miſchiefes of deceiuing
Courtezans.

Written before his death and publiſhed at his
dyeing requeſt.

Fœlicem fuiſſe infauſtum.

LONDON
nprinted for William Wright.
1592.

Table of Contents

Acknowledgements

I am indebted to colleagues Norman Sanders, Tom Wheeler, and Rob Stillman, and students Libby Weatherford and Richard Branyon for generous assistance in many forms; to the Folger Shakespeare Library for permission to use its 1592 quarto as copy-text; to the editors of *Studies in Philology* and *Research Opportunities in Renaissance Drama* for permission to reproduce material, here revised, which appeared first in their journals; to the Trustees of the University of Tennessee Better English Fund, established by John C. Hodges, for financial support during the long period of research; and to my wife, Lisa, for patience, encouragement, and much more.

Preface

Greene's Groatsworth of Wit, entered in the Stationers' Register on 20 September 1592, gave to London the death-bed repentance of Robert Greene, one of its most popular authors and most noted profligates. About two weeks before, Gabriel Harvey had published an account of Greene's sickness and death—how with Thomas Nashe he had indulged in a "fatall banquet of pickle herring," how with a borrowed shirt to his back he had begged in agony for "a penny-pott of Malmsie," and how he was by "his sweete hostisse," Mistress Isam, "for a tender farewell, crowned with a Garland of Bayes: to shew, that a tenth Muse honoured him more being deade; then all the nine honoured him alive."[1] From *Groatsworth* everyone could learn what Greene thought and felt as he died, how his spirit was oppressed by a sense of betrayal and by despair. *Groatsworth* thus completed the life story of a sensitive poet caught between impulse and circumstance, degraded and pitiable, and of a sinner with little hope of escaping eternal punishment. "There have been too many of the Muses' sons whose vices have conducted them to shame and sorrow," wrote his biographer Alexander Dyce in 1831, "but none, perhaps, who have sunk to deeper degradation and misery than the subject of this memoir."[2] *Groatsworth* was, to Charles Knight in 1843, "one of the most extraordinary fragments of autobiography that the vanity or the repentance of a sinful man ever produced."[3]

This is also the pamphlet that gave the world its first published notice of Shakespeare in London: a remarkably bitter outburst against "an upstart Crow, beautified with our feathers," apparently provoked by envy at the success of a player turned playwright. The crossing of these two careers, in the passage with which discussions of Greene end and those of Shakespeare begin, has touched many a sentimentalist as it

---

[1] *Foure Letters and Certeine Sonnets*, ed. G. B. Harrison (1922; repr. New York: Barnes & Noble, 1966), 21, 23.

[2] Ed., *The Dramatic Works of Robert Greene* (London), 1:lxxvi.

[3] Ed., *Comedies, Histories, Tragedies and Poems of William Shakspere* (London), 7:74.

did J. A. Symonds in 1884: "Despicable as were the passions which inspired it, we cannot withhold a degree of pity from the dying Titan, discomfited, undone and superseded, who beheld the young Apollo issue in splendour and awake the world to a new day."[4]

Neither of these motifs emerges from the text in a clear, unambiguous voice. If the book is a death-bed repentance, as it declares itself to be, the tone seems oddly mixed, the malicious zest of the first three quarters being out of keeping with the soulful anguish of the last. And after four centuries there is still no agreement as to the meaning and significance of its attack on Shakespeare. Discussions of these and other troublesome problems have been numerous and widely scattered. I try with each to bring some resolution, even if I cannot completely dispel the mists. On the question of authorship, for example, one of the most vexing of these problems, I show that the case for a serious participation by Henry Chettle is much stronger than has been generally thought. Greene *may* have had something to do with the writing of *Groatsworth*, Chettle *certainly* did. If the book is indeed Chettle's, or largely his, as few have believed and as the evidence seems to suggest, then it ranks as one of the most successful creative hoaxes in our culture.

---

[4] *Shakspere's Predecessors in the English Drama* (repr. London, 1900), 440.

Introduction

Authorship, Circumstances of Publication, Sources and Influences, Date

Groatsworth should not be described, simply, as "by Robert Greene." It was indeed printed in 1592 as *Greenes, Groats-worth of Witte* and advertised as "Written before his death and published at his dyeing request." It also reflects notions widespread at that time about the kind of life he led and, after the point when it shifts from third to first person, conveys a pathos Greene could well have experienced and recorded just before dying. Parts of it resemble episodes in specific works by him, and it shares with his work in general a stock of words and allusions. But there are serious questions about its authenticity that rise out of certain features of the text, its unusual circumstances of publication, and early reactions to it. These questions involve the role of the man who acknowledged having prepared it for the press, Henry Chettle, a printer of limited means who occasionally turned his hand to writing. The evidence suggests that Chettle had much more to do with the book than he admitted and more than has been generally realized since then. Exactly how much more is impossible to tell. Either Chettle cobbled together (with some rather strenuous editing) material by himself, possibly Greene, and even, perhaps, someone else, so that the book is the result of collaboration, or else he wrote it all himself and did so in a way that would make it appear to be Greene's. The evidence is not quite such that the book should be proclaimed an outright forgery, relieving Greene of any part at all, but it certainly inclines that way.

Important evidence comes from matter preliminary to three books published soon after *Groatsworth*, which was entered on 20 September 1592. In the preface to his *Kind-Heart's Dream*, entered on 8 December 1592, Chettle categorically denies having authored it. Greene left "many papers in sundry Booke sellers hands," he tells us, "among

other his Groats-worth of wit."[5] It "was all *Greenes*," he insists,
neither his own nor, as some had "unjustly" charged, Thomas
Nashe's. He recounts his role precisely: "I had onely in the copy this
share, it was il written, as sometimes *Greenes* hand was none of the
best, licensd it must be, ere it could bee printed which could never be
if it might not be read. To be breife I writ it over, and as neare as I
could, followed the copy, onely in that letter I put something out, but
in the whole booke not a worde in." Scholars suspect that what he
removed from the letter to the fellow playwrights—which, "had it
beene true, yet to publish it, was intollerable"—referred to Christopher Marlowe's homosexuality or else his blasphemy. The sole point
of Chettle's preface, since it says nothing else and he had not intended to identify himself as *Kind-Heart's* author (otherwise "it had come
forth without a father"), was to deny that he had written *Groatsworth*.

Chettle's defense was obviously prompted by serious rumors. In
the epistle to the second edition of *Pierce Penniless*, which R. B.
McKerrow thought was issued by mid-October, Nashe regrets not
having had an opportunity in the first edition to inform Greene's
ghost of "what a coyle there is with pamphleting on him after his
death."[6] Nashe refers, presumably, to Gabriel Harvey's letters and
sonnets, in part about Greene, which appeared within days of
Greene's death: the second letter, published first and separately, *Three
Letters, and Certain Sonnets*, and *Four Letters, and Certain Sonnets*.[7]
But Nashe's remark may easily be taken to refer also to the first and
perhaps the second of the only other pamphlets about Greene to
survive from that period, *Groatsworth* and *The Repentance of Robert
Greene*, the latter entered 6 October. If so, then Greene, he is suggesting, had nothing to do with them. *Groatsworth* he goes on to call
"a scald trivial lying pamphlet," which seems a particularly harsh way
to describe the work of a friend or acquaintance. Certainly the force

---

[5] Ed. G. B. Harrison (New York: E. P. Dutton, 1923), 5–7. In quotations
from early books, features no longer common (ampersands, ligatures, swash
letters, and so on) are modernized. Dates of entry are from *A Transcript of the
Registers of the Company of Stationers of London, 1554–1640*, ed. Edward Arber, 5
vols. (London, 1875–94).

[6] *The Works of Thomas Nashe*, ed. R. B. McKerrow (1904–10; rev. Oxford:
Blackwell, 1958), 1:153–54. McKerrow discusses the date of the second edition
of *Pierce* at 4:79.

[7] On the publications of Harvey's Letters, see McKerrow, ed., *Nashe*, 4:152–
53; F. R. Johnson, "The First Edition of Gabriel Harvey's *Foure Letters*," *Library*,
ser. 4, no. 15 (1934): 212–23; "Gabriel Harvey's *Three Letters*: A First Issue of his
Foure Letters," *Library*, ser 5, no. 2 (1946): 135–36; Janet E. Biller, "Gabriel
Harvey's *Foure Letters* (1592): A Critical Edition," (unpubl. Ph.D. diss., Columbia Univ., 1969).

with which he denies any role for himself carries conviction: "God never have care of my soule, but utterly renounce me, if the least word or sillable in it proceeded from my pen, or if I were any way privie to the writing or printing of it." If Nashe knew who wrote it (he was probably in the country when it appeared), then he held his peace. He may have wanted to protect Chettle, who seems to have been his friend, or himself, given some of his own dealings with printers. Despite his claim to the contrary in this epistle, Nashe may have known about the printing of the first edition of *Pierce*, entered on 8 August, which contains some inflammatory matter.[8]

In this preface to *Kind-Heart's*, Chettle makes a surprising confession. He admits that it was he, not Nashe, who wrote the epistle to the second part of Anthony Munday's *Gerileon*, entered on 8 August 1592. Perhaps Chettle meant a confession and explanation in the case of this minor fraud to strengthen his defense against the more serious charge. (An anxious Nashe may have forced the confession.) But one can from it move toward the opposite conclusion, which makes Chettle capable of both fraud and prevarication. His claim that the compositors of *Gerileon* supplied the initials "T. N." in error is questioned by C. T. Wright, in view of Chettle's long acquaintance with the "workman" in question, Thomas Scarlet, whom he may even have helped with the printing.[9] Anyone who reads the epistle can see that Chettle attempts to pass it off as Nashe's. "T. N." opens the epistle with a heavy reference to his absence: "Absence, among approoved frends, dissevers not affect, neither can the change of aire change resolved minds. In absence . . . ," and so on. Nashe was away from London on 8 August because of the plague; there is no evidence of Chettle's absence. Harold Jenkins, who accepts Chettle's explanation, excuses the printers because the style is so like Nashe's, as indeed it is.[10] What we have in this epistle, surely, is a hoax, carried out in the month before *Groatsworth* was published, one that illustrates Chettle's competence at and impulse toward imitation, and one that resulted in an attempt on his part at a cover up. Several verbal

---

[8] Peter Alexander (*Introductions to Shakespeare* [New York: Norton, 1964], 128) thought Nashe's remarks acknowledge that *Groatsworth* may not have been Greene's. Nashe maligning a book Chettle wrote could explain (no other explanation has been put forth) why Harvey accused Nashe of "odiously" misusing Chettle (*Works of Gabriel Harvey*, ed. A. B. Grosart [1844; repr. New York: AMS, 1966], 2:322). Both Nashe and Chettle deny Harvey's charge without saying what it is, in a letter Nashe quotes as Chettle's (*Nashe*, 3:131).

[9] "Mundy and Chettle in Grub Street," *Boston University Studies in English* 5 (1961): 131.

[10] *The Life and Work of Henry Chettle* (London: Sidgwick & Jackson, 1934), 14.

links between the *Gerileon* epistle and *Groatsworth* suggest Chettle's hand in *Groatsworth*.[11]

Chettle's admission of having edited something out of the Marlowe section does not sound invented. But if as an afterthought Chettle had edited himself, then the excision would have been evident to printer, publisher, or registrar, and so could easily be, perhaps had to be, acknowledged. Obviously under stress, Chettle makes a series of minor admissions in this preface: he was responsible for printing the attack on Shakespeare; he wrote an epistle which got printed over someone else's initials; he was about to publish a book (*Kind-Heart's*) without acknowledging his authorship (we may infer that he had done this sort of thing before); and he was responsible for the peculiar fact that the *Groatsworth* manuscript was not in Greene's hand (the original was apparently missing). Someone knew, or could learn from the printers or registrar, that a manuscript by Greene was not available. We have no evidence to help us decide whether Greene's handwriting was bad enough to require a fair copy.

If Chettle wrote *Groatsworth*, he could not simply admit it. There could be serious troubles with the authorities over the beast fable called "*Lamilias Fable*," which, as we shall see, is a veiled attack against Lord Burghley, the seriousness of which cannot be overestimated. Admission might also jeopardize his position as writer for the players attacked (he seems already to have been affiliated with the theater) or, perhaps, his chances of getting work or of recovering work lost because of the closing of the theaters or the ascendancy of Shakespeare. We can certainly wonder about Chettle's expression: "I am as sory," he says of the Shakespeare attack, "as if the originall fault had beene my fault." In view of other grounds for suspicion, this may appear self-implicating. Does the forger, like the plagiarist, seek,

---

[11] From the epistle's two and a half pages (STC 17206, A4–A5), compare "you will make no doubt" with "I will make no doubt" (lines 75–76), "go forward with my purpose" with "Ile forward with my tale" (lines 436–37), "Arch-workmaister" with "Arch-plaimaking-poet" (line 715), "sea-swolne" with "like the sea somtime sweld" (lines 715–16), "had saved his owne" with "the Gentleman saved his owne" (line 752), "some wainscot fac'd fellowe" with "his new turnd face, . . . of wainscot proofe" (lines 290–91), and "Winter bitter Epitaph" with the "Epitaph" of the grasshopper in winter (line 1018). For possible evidence that Greene did not complete *Groatsworth*, cf. the description of it in the epistle as "like an Embrion without shape" (lines 26–27) with *Nashe*, 3:153–54 (of *Ile of Dogs*): "An imperfect Embrion I may well call it, for I having begun but the induction and first act of it, the other foure acts without my consent, or the least guesse of my drift or scope, by the players were supplied. . . ."

inadvertently or cautiously, to confess or incriminate himself?[12] It may be that Chettle is saying, obliquely and consciously, something like this: "I admit to having written words attributed to Greene, apologize to the one I have wronged, and try to make amends (the extended compliment to Shakespeare), which I trust will do; but for obvious reasons (the potential for trouble with the authorities) I cannot make an open, full confession." Such a reading seems extreme, perhaps unfair, in the face of his unequivocal statement: "onely in that letter I put something out, but in the whole booke not a worde in, for I protest it was all *Greenes*, not mine nor Maister *Nashes*." This claim—"I put . . . not a worde in"—is certainly open to question, as we shall see. Chettle may have been caught in a difficult position. That the wording of his apology (". . . as if the originall fault had beene my fault") can suggest self-incrimination, if such is the case, may for some, however, testify as to its ingenuousness.

Among those who suspected Chettle, it is clear from his preface, were Shakespeare and Marlowe. "[O]ne or two," he says, having taken offense at the letter to the playwrights, "because on the dead they cannot be avenged, . . . wilfully forge in their conceites a living Author: and after tossing it two and fro, no remedy, but it must light on me." These two, we may assume, would want to know who wrote it and would be capable, even if we ourselves are not, of detecting a fault.[13]

That there were questions about the posthumous Greene pamphlets we also know from a third printed reaction (after Chettle's and Nashe's): the publisher's epistle to *Greene's Vision*, also published late in 1592 (this one unregistered) in order to capitalize on Greene's notoriety and demise and "Written at the instant of his *death*" (title page). "Manie have published repentaunces under his name," Thomas Newman declares, "but none more unfeigned than this, being everie word of his owne: his own phrase, his own method." Newman must refer to *Groatsworth* and *The Repentance* ("*repentaunces*"). It sounds as though he implies, based on what he knows or suspects (or knows others suspect), that Chettle himself participated seriously in the making of *Groatsworth*, and in such a way as to be able to call it

---

[12] See Peter Shaw on the urge to confess, in "Plagiary," *American Scholar* 15 (1982): 325–37.

[13] Some have thought Shakespeare not one of those who took offense: Howard Staunton, letter in *Athenaeum*, 7 Feb. 1874, 193–94; F. G. Fleay, *Life and Work of William Shakespeare* (London, 1886), 111; W. H. Chapman, *William Shakspere and Robert Greene: The Evidence* (1912; repr. New York: Haskell House, 1974), 71ff.

Greene's even though, essentially, it was not. Newman may not, of course, be trustworthy, since it would be to his advantage to diminish the authenticity of the earlier books. The title page promotion for his own book, incidentally, misleads about as much as Chettle's preface might. The text of *Greene's Vision* is indeed Greene's—but what Newman does not say is that the book itself was written much earlier, in 1590, which we can readily deduce from internal evidence. The only justification for his claim is a two-page epistle signed "*Yours dying*: Robert Greene," the authenticity of which one may legitimately doubt.[14]

The first modern to suspect Chettle was the great forger himself, John Payne Collier, in a note to his 1844 *Life of William Shakespeare*.[15] Perhaps "it takes a forger to expose a fake" (a motto, Anthony Grafton says in *Forgers and Critics*, that ought to hang on the wall of every literary detective's study[16]). Collier, with reason, no doubt, did not repeat his suspicion.[17] A sustained case for Chettle as author or co-author was published in 1933 by C. E. Sanders, who also argued against the genuineness of *The Repentance*. But any influence Sanders might have had was immediately offset by Harold

---

[14] *The Life and Complete Works in Prose and Verse of Robert Greene*, ed. A. B. Grosart, 15 vols. (London, 1881–86), 12:193, 196. In the end of *Vision* (274) Greene asks us to "looke as speedily as the presse wil serve for my mourning garment." The *Mourning Garment* was entered on 2 November 1590 and printed in that year. One of J. Churton Collins' three scenarios has the *Visions* epistle a forgery (ed., *The Plays & Poems of Robert Greene*, 2 vols. [Oxford: Clarendon, 1905], 1:126 n.); J. C. Jordan thinks it genuine (*Robert Greene* [New York: Columbia Univ. Press, 1915], 169); René Pruvost and Charles W. Crupi have serious doubts (*Robert Greene et Ses Romans (1558–1592)* [Paris: Belles Lettres, 1938], 369; *Robert Greene* [Boston: Twayne, 1986], 35), as do I.

[15] *The Works of William Shakespeare* (London), 1:cxxxi, n.: "We have some doubts about the authenticity of the 'Groats-worth of Witte' as a work by Greene. Chettle was a needy dramatist, and possibly wrote it in order to avail himself of the high popularity of Greene. . . . Falling into some discredit, in consequence of the publication of it, Chettle reasserted that it was by Greene."

[16] (Princeton: Princeton Univ. Press, 1990), 123.

[17] A few since have thought forgery probable: Theodore Vetter, "Robert Greene und seine Prosa," *Verhandlungen der 44. Versammlung deutscher Philologen und Schulmänner*, ed. Reinhard Albrecht (Leipzig, 1897), 147–51; J. M. Manly, *English Prose (1137–1890)* (Boston: Ginn, 1909), xvi; Florence Trotter, "*Greenes Groatsworth of Wit*," unpubl. M. A. thesis, Univ. of Chicago, 1912; W. H. Chapman, *William Shakspere and Robert Greene*, 86–91, for whom the famous letter was the only part by Greene. W. A. Jackson (*The Carl H. Pforzheimer Library* [New York: privately printed, 1940], 2:415) thought it "possible to make a fairly convincing argument against the attribution of this work to Greene."

Jenkins' rebuttal in 1935.[18] Since then, scholars, usually glancing in the direction of the doubts, have maintained the Greene attribution. Some willingness to entertain question followed Warren B. Austin's 1969 study based on a computer comparison of styles, which concluded that Chettle alone could have been the author.[19] For Samuel Schoenbaum, who is careful in such matters, despite "traces of unease" over Chettle's apologia, Austin did not prove his case, and so it has been for others.[20] Not any single piece of evidence for Chettle's participation is, of itself, very significant: it is the large quantity and wide variety that matter.

∽

Several passages in *Groatsworth* arouse suspicion. First, its account of Roberto's career as playwright seems to depend on Gabriel Harvey's second letter, published soon after 5 September (when it is dated) to take advantage of the news of Greene's death, on 2 or 3 September.[21] The letter's account of the life and death of the "famous Author" who had "notoriously grown a very proverbe of Infamy, and contempt" reflected and in turn helped create a demand for material on Greene. These two accounts, Harvey's and *Groatsworth's*, both brief, make the same kinds of generalizations and share words and details. Both describe his poverty, his irresponsible pamphleting, and his vile company. In the second letter, we have his "continuall shifting of lodginges, . . . his beggarly departing in every hostisses debt." In *Groatsworth*, we have his "shift of lodgings, where in every place his Hostesse writ up the wofull remembrance of him" (lines 723–25). Both give his associations with the criminal Cutting

---

[18] "Robert Greene and His 'Editors,'" *PMLA* 48 (1933): 392–417; "On the Authenticity of *Greene's Groatsworth of Wit* and *The Repentance of Robert Greene*," *Review of English Studies* 11 (1935): 28–41.

[19] *A Computer-Aided Technique for Stylistic Discrimination: The Authorship of "Greene's Groats-worth of Wit."* Project BR-7-G-036, U.S. Department of H.E.W. (Washington, D.C.: U.S. Office of Education). Barbara Kreifelts' 1972 dissertation at the Univ. of Cologne, *Eine statistische Stilanalyse zur Klärung von Autorenschaftsfragen, durchgeführt am Beispiel von "Greens Groatsworth of Wit"* (129 pp.), using a different computer method, also finds Chettle the likely author.

[20] *William Shakespeare: A Documentary Life* (New York: Oxford Univ. Press, 1975), 118–19. The reviews are listed, below, in note 76.

[21] The second letter dated 5 September has "hys buriall yesterday" (*Foure Letters*, ed. Harrison, 22). Since in plague time burial was hasty, 3 September seems a good guess for his death. Harvey's account of the circumstances of Greene's death, despite Nashe's effort at denial, has been accepted as probably true; E. H. Miller calls it "devastatingly accurate" (*Professional Writer in Elizabethan England* [Cambridge, MA: Harvard Univ. Press, 1959], 157).

Ball and Ball's sister (whom Greene is "keping" in one, "kept" in the other), and both allude to Ball's hanging: in the second letter "he was intercepted at Tiborne" and his crew are "his trustiest companions"; in *Groatsworth* he is "trust under a tree as round as a Ball" (lines 742–43). We can believe that if Harvey learned Chettle had a manuscript (even that Chettle was creating one) he would have taken quick steps to see it, given Greene's abuse of the Harvey family in *A Quip for an Upstart Courtier* in July. A Harvey debt to Greene, of course, would be an argument for the existence of *Groatsworth* at the time of Greene's death. But Harvey would have had almost no time to see it before composing his letter, assuming that the manuscript was with Greene at the time of his death, unless Harvey saw it when he visited Mrs. Isam's after Greene's death. The letter to his wife in *Groatsworth* is described as *"founde with this booke after his death."* The text of *Groatsworth* wants us to believe that it was with Greene: "Now faint I of my last infirmity, beseeching them that shall burie my bodie, to publish this last farewell written with my wretched hand" (lines 1042–44). (Chettle's preface to *Kind-Heart's* seems ambiguous on this point: compare "About three moneths since died *M. Robert Greene*, leaving many papers in sundry Booke sellers hands, among other his Groats-worth of wit.") It is unlikely that Harvey could have seen it by 5 September, that is, over two weeks before 20 September, when it was registered. Nor was the section at issue printed in Wolfe's shop, where Harvey resided. The account in *Groatsworth* that seems to depend on Harvey, we should note, occurs in the text where some "editing" might have been necessary if Chettle was dealing with fragments, just before the shift in point of view and mode. The second letter also seems to anticipate (perhaps to have influenced) *Groatsworth*'s "yong *Juvenall*" section: its "his [Greene's] fellow-writer, a proper yong man if advised in time" suggests *Groatsworth*'s "yong" and "might I advise thee, be advisde" (lines 917–19).[22]

 Groatsworth's account of Greene's life, it seems fair to say, provides little that is personal in detail or attitude, little that could not have

---

[22] *Foure Letters*, ed. Harrison, 13–14, 19–21. There are other, lesser verbal parallels, noted in the commentary. C. M. Ingleby, apparently without realizing that the dates conflicted, gave ways he thought Harvey's third letter, dated 8 and 9 September, retaliated against *Groatsworth*, in *Shakspere Allusion-Books* (London, 1874), pt. 1, xxvii–viii. The commentary also notes ten parallels between *Groatsworth* and Nashe's *Pierce*, published a few days *after* Greene's death, though entered on 8 August (McKerrow, ed., *Nashe*, 4:78). None is strong enough to require a connection, though taken together they suggest one. Harvey had not seen *Pierce* when he wrote his second letter; he discusses it in his third letter.

derived from Greene's published books or his general notoriety.[23] We do not, of course, expect its prodigal son story to fit Greene's life exactly—his father to have been a usurer, he the eldest of two sons and disinherited. As for its expression, Greene may have written almost all of it early on, before he was sick enough to voice something other than the conventional, generalized patterns of remorse and resolution. He may even have found comfort toward the end in old, stylized forms. Still, at and after the moment when the prodigal son story gives way and we are brought up to the present with Roberto in London, just before the fragments, which are contemplative rather than narrative, we expect something more than, or different from, what we know already from other sources. The anecdote of the gentleman falsely accused of stealing a ring (lines 744ff.), which sounds like an actual incident, and the letter to the playwrights, with its outburst against Shakespeare, might weaken this argument for Chettle. Our disappointment, in any case, may reflect modern notions of what autobiography is. No serious history of the genre includes *Groatsworth* in its discussion.

Second, we are expected to believe that the Greene who writes the epistle *"To the Gentlemen Readers"* does so at some point *before* he finishes *Groatsworth* ("If I live to end it . . ."), even, perhaps, *before* he starts it, a procedure very unlikely at the time. Furthermore, even as the epistle firmly anticipates his death, expressing the fear that it will soon take place, it nevertheless promises, incredibly, that should he

---

[23] Sanders, in "Greene and His 'Editors,' " 397–98, discusses this point. On Greene's life the best place to begin is Crupi's *Robert Greene* and follow his references, especially Brenda Richardson, "Robert Greene's Yorkshire Connexions: A New Hypothesis," *Year's Work in English Studies* 10 (1980): 160–80. Richardson thinks it unlikely that the Norwich saddler Robert Greene who may have had only two sons is the poet's father, though she admits that there is other evidence for him. The fact that the other Robert Greene, the Norwich innkeeper, does not mention the poet in his will she takes to reflect the possibility, suggested by *Groatsworth*, that Greene was disinherited. The Roberto story actually conforms generally to the life of Thomas Lodge. He was involved in suits with his brothers over an inheritance, had a father who held office in the city (as alderman and Lord Mayor) and had cut him off, went to university, wrote plays, and was famous about the city as a prodigal. Roberto's origins appear to be in London, not Norwich. Too, Chettle or Greene may have had Lodge manuscripts on hand (while Lodge was away at sea), since Chettle entered Lodge's *Catharos* in 1591 and Greene prepared for press *Euphues' Shadow* (ent. 17 February 1592). For C. J. Sisson (*Thomas Lodge and Other Elizabethans* [1933; repr. New York: Octagon, 1966], 103), "the life of Francesco or of Roberto, as Greene narrates it, is in essentials the life at this period of Lodge, the companion of Greene and Nashe." The Roberto story may have originally been, up to the break, modeled on Lodge's; it may have even been by Lodge.

survive, he will supply more of the very works ("directing you how to live, yet not diswading ye from love") that in the book, in the face of the likelihood of death, he absolutely condemns. One way to explain these peculiarities is to believe Greene wrote the epistle *after* he knew that he was ill but *before* he knew he was critically so, that is, just as he resumed work on a story begun some time before. The first three quarters of *Groatsworth*, it should be noted, give no indication whatsoever that its hero Roberto is or will be ill or in any danger of death. And yet at the moment when we learn that Roberto is sick, at the break, when "Roberto" becomes "I" (line 781), when Greene might have resumed writing, then we know that he is sick unto death. Suggesting as it does that Greene *might* die, the epistle reflects an attitude present in neither of the two parts of *Groatsworth*. If Greene had finished the book, he would have written the epistle last. In my own view, the epistle, though it attempts to disguise the matter, is informed by a certainty that Greene will die. Even if Chettle had some material from Greene, he probably had no epistle. Greene's works always carried one by him, and Chettle, as with the epistle to *Gerileon*, may have been reluctant to sign one himself. Too much of the credibility and power of the conclusion, which implies that Greene is dying, would be lost by having a revived Greene introduce the completed work. Chettle thus had Greene introduce it and do so at some point before he had finished it, relying, perhaps, on the naive readers' sense that what comes first is written first or early on.

Third, "*A letter written to his wife, founde with this booke after his death*" (lines 1046ff.), which serves as a sort of appendix, is suspect. It bears no resemblance to either of the two other letters that the dying Greene is supposed to have written to her, the one Harvey quotes, apparently from memory, in the second letter as having been "kindly shewed" to him by Mrs. Isam, who nursed Greene, the other quoted by Cuthbert Burby as being "to this effect," not saying how he came by it, in *The Repentance*.[24] Both of these, unlike that in the *Groatsworth*, are short and ask that his wife pay his debt to his host. The relationship between these two we can only guess at. Burby's, published later than Harvey's, looks like either a refined version of Harvey's or else what Harvey actually saw and tried to recreate. To accept our letter as authentic we must assume the existence of (at least) two letters, to be explained by a theory like that of Jenkins, who thinks the *Groatsworth* letter, which is more formal and less urgent

---

[24] *Foure Letters*, ed. Harrison, 22; *The Repentance of Robert Greene*, ed. G. B. Harrison (1923; repr. New York: Barnes & Noble, 1966), 32.

than the others, was written sometime earlier and not yet posted.[25] Given its impersonal, careful style, Florence Trotter wonders whether its author was "more concerned with euphonic effect than with the matter."[26] The major difficulty, however, concerns the child Greene returned with the letter to its mother, Greene's estranged wife. Now Harvey says that Greene had with him at his death the mother, Cutting Ball's sister, of his "base sonne" named "Infortunatus," and we know a Fortunatus Greene was buried in Shoreditch on 12 August 1593.[27] *Groatsworth* says that "his laundresse, and his boy" (line 725) were ever with him, which does not resolve the problem. Unless Greene, after about six years in which he had not seen his wife, had the keep of his legitimate child, and Harvey was simply wrong, or of both children, neither of which conditions seems at all likely, our writer confuses the two children. On such grounds both Jenkins and René Pruvost had doubts as to the letter's authenticity.[28]

Fourth, two of the plays listed by *Groatsworth*'s Player-Patron as part of his old-fashioned repertory seem to be among those listed by the Players as part of theirs in *The Book of Sir Thomas More—Groatsworth*: "twas I that pende the Morrall of mans witte, the Dialogue of Dives" (lines 674–75); *More*: "dives and Lazarus, . . . and the mariage of witt and wisedome."[29] John Jowett assigns the *More* scene to Chettle "with little fear of contradiction," and it is thought written in the hand of Munday, Chettle's friend.[30] Incidentally, many who have studied Chettle's contribution to *More* (thought to be Hand A) agree that he probably collaborated with Munday (Hand S) sometime in the spring or summer of 1592. If we need a motive for the outburst

---

[25] Jenkins, "Authenticity," 34.

[26] *"Greenes Groatsworth of Wit,"* 25.

[27] *Foure Letters*, ed. Harrison, 20; note also 21, 22, and 33. John Payne Collier announced the discovery in *Memoirs of the Principal Actors in the Plays of Shakespeare* (London, 1846), xx.

[28] "Authenticity," 34–35; *Robert Greene*, 514–15. Trotter, *"Greenes Groatsworth of Wit,"* 25, suspects it; Collins, ed., *Plays & Poems*, 1:46–47, 52, thinks a copy of the *Groatsworth* letter must have been sent to the wife; Sanders, "Greene and His 'Editors,' " 397–98, 410, dismisses it. Cf. Nashe on Harvey's letter: "For . . . sending that miserable writte to his wife, it cannot be but that thou lyest, learned *Gabriel"* (*Nashe*, 1:287). Greene's mistress in *Never Too Late* declares herself with child. Philomela, in the work of that name entered 1 July 1592 but "written long since," has a child named Infortunatus.

[29] *The Book of Sir Thomas More*, lines 118–22, ed. W. W. Greg ([Oxford:] Malone Society, 1911), 31.

[30] "Henry Chettle and the Original Text of *Sir Thomas More*," in *Shakespeare and "Sir Thomas More,"* ed. T. H. Howard-Hill (Cambridge: Cambridge Univ. Press, 1989), 147.

against Shakespeare other than the obvious one of wanting to appear
to be Greene, then we may suspect something growing out of the
work on *More*. The scenario suggested by Peter W. M. Blayney and
Scott McMillin dates Shakespeare's addition to *More* (Hand D) in
late 1592 and defines his task as being to supplement (refashion or
complete) work already begun or done by Munday and Chettle—
work the two may well have considered their own.[31] If such was the
case, Chettle may have felt some animus toward Shakespeare, whom he
had not met. By the time he writes the preface to *Kind-Heart's*,
however, that is, by 8 December, he has himself "seene [Shake-
speare's] demeanor no lesse civill than he exelent in the qualitie he
professes: Besides, divers of worship have reported . . . his facetious
grace in writting, that approoves his Art." With Greene's friends no
longer writing plays, which is what the letter advises, the field would
be left, as indeed happened, to those without university training, to
Munday and Chettle.

↫

Before turning to general matters of content and style it seems
advisable to present the remaining external evidence for a Chettle
participation. It is true that Chettle, like many another who wrote,
wrote to live. But his need seems to have been intense, and what is
more important, he, along with others in his set, explicitly apologized
for indiscretions in print or having to do with printing on grounds of
need. Greene was so popular that anything with his name on it was
certain to sell. All other works have grown "out of request," Harvey
lamented in the very month Chettle was generating the text, "and the
Countesse of Pembrookes Arcadia is not greene inough for queasie
stomackes, but they must have *Greenes* Arcadia: and I beleeve most
eagerlie longed for *Greenes* Faerie Queene."[32] Chettle had no steady
source of income, no shop of his own. He seems to have relied on the
odd composing job and literary grubwork. Riots against strangers in
the late spring of 1592, which closed the theaters, reflected the dire
economic conditions in London. The spread of the plague in the late

---

[31] See the summary of scholarship by G. Harold Metz, in *Shakespeare and
"Sir Thomas More,"* esp. 25–26; Blayney, *"The Booke of Sir Thomas Moore*
Re-Examined," *Studies in Philology* 69 (1972): 167–91; McMillin, *The Elizabethan
Theatre and "The Book of Sir Thomas More"* (Ithaca: Cornell Univ. Press, 1987),
145–51. After presenting in some detail the "story" of Munday, Chettle, and
Shakespeare working on *More* in 1592, McMillin has it "almost bound to be
untrue" because its "every element is hedged with doubt." Still, he is much taken
with it.
[32] *Foure Letters*, ed. Harrison, 41.

summer and fall must have restricted his chances for work. He cannot have been much better off than he was a few years later, during the time of his relationship with Henslowe, when Harold Jenkins has him in a state of "constant impecuniosity."[33] In *Kind-Heart's Dream*, entered 8 December, Chettle (as Kind-Heart) would readily take on himself the challenge Greene's ghost gives to Pierce Penniless (Nashe) for revenge against the Harveys, "for in my life I was not more pennilesse than at that instant," that is, in September, the "instant" of Harvey's attack on Greene and the production of *Groatsworth*.[34] This particular remark of Chettle's sounds like an apology or explanation for *Groatsworth*. He evidently considered poverty sufficient to account for, perhaps to excuse, the most celebrated libel of the day, Greene's abuse of the Harveys in *A Quip for an Upstart Courtier*, entered 21 July 1592. "But for my povertie," he has Greene's ghost in *Kind-Heart's* say, "meethinkes wisedome would have brideled that invective."[35] Even Harvey allows financial need as excuse when, in Sonnet XVIII, published with his letters in mid-September, he has his brother welcome Greene to the grave with "I pardon thy offence to me: / It was thy living."[36] Whoever wrote the epistle to *Greene's Vision* over Greene's name offers the same defense: "Many things I have wrote to get money, which I could otherwise wish to be supprest: Povertie is the father of innumerable infirmities."[37] Nashe, in response to Harvey's charge that "like a Curtizan" he prostituted his pen, thought a plea of poverty answer enough.[38] The most dignified use of this plea had been made by John Wolfe, in the spring of 1588, when questioned as to why he printed books belonging to another: "Because," he replied, "I will live."[39]

If he forged it, Chettle may have been inspired by printed reactions to Richard Tarlton's death, on 3 September 1588, four years to the day before Greene's. A number of edifying "repentances" now lost were attributed to Tarlton. The Register lists, for 23 September 1588, "Tarltons farewell," for 2 August 1589, "Tarltons Recantacon," for 16 October 1589, in anticipation of *Groatsworth*, "Tarltons repentance or his farewell to his frendes in his sickness a little

---

[33] *Henry Chettle*, 22.
[34] Ed. Harrison, 38.
[35] Ed. Harrison, 36.
[36] *Foure Letters*, ed. Harrison, 98.
[37] *Works*, ed. Grosart, 12:195.
[38] *Nashe*, ed. McKerrow, 3:30.
[39] *Transcript*, ed. Arber, 2:780.

before his deathe."[40] Printed reactions to the Tarlton-Greene deaths ran parallel: consider *Tarlton's News Out of Purgatory*, entered 26 June 1590, and B. R.'s *Greene's News Both From Heaven and Hell*, entered 3 February 1593. Greene was certainly associated with Tarlton in the popular mind, as we know from Harvey's pairing of their names. Greene may even have taken up with Tarlton's mistress.[41] Moreover, the mood and substance of the last quarter of *Groatsworth*, which are quite conventional, conform to that large body of popular literature of death and confession much of which, as M. A. Shaaber has described it, is of doubtful authority. It presents, especially, the recantations of Catholics or of criminals, and consists chiefly of lamentation, repentance, and exhortation to the reader to avoid evil courses. Two special features typical of this literature, according to Shaaber, are that it is written in the first person (like the last quarter of *Groatsworth*) and purports to be the speaker's own words written just before his death.[42]

What we know about others involved in *Groatsworth*'s publication, while it produces no firm evidence, might provoke question. John Danter, who printed half of it (sheets D-F), has come down to us as the type of the unscrupulous printer. In W. W. Greg's words, "[his career] is nothing but a record of piracy and secret printing, from the time he infringed his master's rights during apprenticeship to the time

---

[40] *Transcript*, ed. Arber, 2:500, 526, 531.

[41] *Foure Letters*, ed. Harrison, 18–19, 52. M. C. Bradbrook notices that connections were made between the two. She observes, incidentally, that Will Kemp objected to ballad singers foisting ballads upon him, in *Rise of the Common Player* (Cambridge, MA: Harvard Univ. Press, 1962), 163ff., 305n. Mark Eccles presents the evidence that Tarlton died in the house of Em Ball, later Greene's mistress, in *Christopher Marlowe in London* (Cambridge, MA: Harvard Univ. Press, 1934), 124–26. Greene himself almost certainly engaged in literary hoaxes. E. H. Miller makes a good case for him, with the possible help of Nashe, as author of *The Defence of Cony-Catching*, by "Cuthbert Conny-catcher"; see *Notes and Queries* 196 (1951): 509–12; 197 (1952): 446–51; *Philological Quarterly* 33 (1954): 358–62; David Parker, *Notes and Queries* 219 (1974): 87–89. Charles Nicholl, in *A Cup of News: The Life of Thomas Nashe* (London: Routledge & Kegan Paul, 1984), 125–30, makes a similar case, apparently unaware of Miller's views. Many have expressed suspicions, including Pruvost, in *Robert Greene*, 445–47. In *Greene's Vision* (12:197–98), Greene complained that some held him responsible for the anonymous *Cobbler of Canterbury* (1590), as several modern scholars have (see H. Neville Davies' edition [Cambridge, 1976], 29–30). D. N. Ranson believes Greene wrote *Tarlton's News* (1590); see his edition of 1974.

[42] *Some Forerunners of the Newspaper in England, 1476–1622* (Philadelphia: Univ. of Penn. Press, 1929), 98, 143–44.

he disappears in disgrace from the records of the Company."[43] In *Greene's Funerals*, largely by "R. B.," probably Richard Barnfield, but brought together and printed by Danter (ent. in 1594) "contrarie to the Authours expectation," appears the startling claim, Danter's presumably, that two sets of verses by the Catholic Richard Stanyhurst were quoted by Greene *"at the instant of his death."* The very idea, in R. B. McKerrow's summary judgment, "has about it a certain grotesqueness."[44] (This book, though entered in 1594, was probably finished in September 1592.) Danter apparently had no inhibitions. Nor had Wolfe, who printed the other half (A–C), whose press was voracious, and who, in the words of the most recent student of his career, "may rank as one of his culture's greatest sneaks."[45] William Wright, the publisher of *Groatsworth*, was of Wolfe's party in rebelling against the copyright privileges of established printers. He was master of Burby, freed in January 1592, another printing opportunist. Burby published both Munday's *Gerileon* in 1592 with the false ascription to the epistle by Chettle and *The Repentance* (printed by Danter), the authenticity of which has been seriously questioned.[46] It was Burby who in 1592 published *Axiochus* as translated by "Edward Spenser" when it is likely that the work was by someone else, probably Anthony Munday. Danter

---

[43] *Two Elizabethan Stage Abridgements: "The Battle of Alcazar" & "Orlando Furioso"* (Oxford: Oxford Univ. Press for the Malone Society, 1922), 130. Sidney Thomas, in *Studies in Bibliography* 19 (1966): 196–97, shows that *Groatsworth* was printed by Danter and Wolfe; W. A. Jackson had said so in *Pforzheimer Catalogue* (1940), 2:415. For the publishing history of Greene's works, see A. F. Allison's *Robert Greene (1558–1592): A Bibliographical Catalogue of the Early Editions in English (To 1640)* (Folkestone, Kent: Dawson, 1975).

[44] *"Greenes Newes both from Heaven and Hell" and "Greenes Funeralls,"* ed. McKerrow (1911; repr. Stratford-upon-Avon: Shakespeare Head, 1922), 69, 86–87, viii.

[45] Joseph Lowenstein, "For a History of Literary Property: John Wolfe's Reformation," *English Literary Renaissance* 18 (1988): 390.

[46] By Sanders, in the 1933 *PMLA* article. Among those who have doubted its authenticity Sanders cites (404) K. F. Bodenstet (1860), Dyce (1861), who later changed his mind, Collier (1862), W. C. Hazlitt (1867), and Hermann Ulrici (1868). Collins (ed., *Plays & Poems* [1905], 1:52), was "half inclined" to find in it something of the missing repentance volume, the part registered but not printed (see note 49 below). Norbert Bolz concludes that Greene had no part in it in *Eine statistische, computerunterstützte Echtheitsprüfung von "The Repentance of Robert Greene": Ein methodischer und systematischer Ansatz* (Frankfurt am Main: Peter Lang, 1978). He gives an English summary in *Shakespeare Newsletter* 29 (Dec. 1979): 43. Greene cannot have had much, if anything, to do with it.

probably printed part of it.[47] Newman, who published *Greene's Vision*, was responsible for the 1591 *Astrophel and Stella*, a book impounded by the authorities for its irregularities. A recent study has it that Newman "betrayed every poet represented in his publication."[48] Little about this network inspires confidence in attributions.

As for Greene's dealings with the two who matter, Chettle and Danter, the evidence is scanty. Nothing else clearly connects Greene with Chettle, though they could have known each other, especially if Chettle had already worked as a dramatist. In view of Chettle's open defense of Greene in *Kind-Heart's*, Jenkins deduced that the two were friends. Greene's only possible association with Danter is recorded in an entry made on 21 August, about two weeks before his death, of a book called "The Repentance of a Cony catcher." Chettle, who seems to have kept a low profile, may have procured it. The book as printed by Danter was called *The Black Book's Messenger* and contained only one of the two parts announced in the Register, that of the unrepentant Ned Browne and not that of the repentant Mourton, a change of plan acknowledged in the brief epistle signed by "R. G.," who mentions his sickness. We may surmise that the missing promised portion was never written (it did not emerge as announced), was held back for an unrealized future project, or else, in a theory Churton Collins proposed, Sanders developed, and Jenkins rejected, was adapted to form the posthumous *Repentance*.[49] As for the others, whose roles in *Groatsworth* may have been indirect, in 1592 Wolfe printed numerous Greene works, which is to be expected, and Wright twice published *The Second Part of Cony-Catching*, printed by Wolfe. In 1592, Burby published *The Third and Last Part*.

A mischievous vein seems to have run through Chettle. We have considered the epistle he wrote for *Gerileon* in August 1592 signed "T. N.," which attacks a rival author and publisher who may be Abel

---

[47] The case for someone other than Spenser has won out; see M. W. H. Swan, *English Literary History* 11 (1944): 161–81, who thinks Danter one of the printers. C. T. Wright, in *PMLA* 76 (1961): 34–39, argues that Munday did the translation.

[48] Christopher R. Wilson, "*Astrophil and Stella*: A Tangled Editorial Web," *Library*, ser. 6, vol. 1 (1979): 346.

[49] *Blacke Bookes Messenger*, ed. G. B. Harrison (1924; repr. New York: Barnes & Noble, 1966). The blank where Mourton's first name should be in the Register (ed. Arber, 2:619) suggests that a portion of the book was not delivered for examination. "R. G." announces in the epistle that it "shall shortly be published." See Collins, ed., *Plays & Poems*, 1:52–53; Sanders, "Greene and His 'Editors,' " 407–8; Jenkins, "Authenticity," 36–38. For Jenkins' speculation as to the friendship between Chettle and Greene, see *Henry Chettle*, 8 n.

Jeffes. The ghost of the balladeer "Anthony Now now" in *Kind-Heart's*, in December 1592, seems to be, as C. T. Wright thought he was, an elaborate disguise for Chettle's friend Munday, known for his ballads and very much alive.[50] *Now now* may play on the Latin for *Monday* rendered with a tilde as a kind of plural of *modo: modi*, or *modo . . . modo*, meaning "just now," or two *nows*. And the "Lazarus Pyott" criticized by Chettle as a rival translator to Munday, in a poem and letter of 1596, may be, as M. St. Clare Byrne thought he was, Munday himself.[51] Giorgio Melchiori has shown that some of the old plays listed in *More*, two of which reappear in *Groatsworth* (one on Dives and Lazarus), were connected with the printing shop where Munday and Chettle served together as apprentices.[52] The Player-Patron (who in *Groatsworth* recruits Roberto as a playwright) himself might be Munday, as T. W. Baldwin thought he was, or contain traces of him, which could only be true if the portrait is a playful, inside joke.[53] We might also note that Chettle omitted his name from the title page of Lodge's *Catharos*, which he entered in 1591, perhaps because it contained a good deal of inflammatory matter, including attacks on Burghley and Walsingham.[54] Years later, in 1603, Chettle was quick to exploit another death, that of Elizabeth, with *England's Mourning Garment*.

Chettle may have been uniquely capable of pulling off such a hoax. His training and life experience as a compositor would have taught him skills of memory that, as a would-be writer, he could exploit in imitating the styles of others, and he would have done so

---

[50] *Anthony Mundy: An Elizabethan Man of Letters* (Berkeley: Univ. of California Press, 1928), chap. X; Jenkins did not think so, in *Henry Chettle*, 11–17, 37–38.

[51] Byrne, "Anthony Munday and his Books," *Library*, ser. 4, vol. 1 (1921): 241–42; her argument is impressive. Henry Thomas did not think Munday and "Pyot" the same, in *Spanish and Portuguese Romances of Chivalry* (1920; repr. New York: Kraus, 1969), App. II. "Lazarus" may be based on Munday's translations of continental romances through an allusion to "Lazarillo de Tormes," or on a connection between him and the Dives and Lazarus motif, on which see Appendix D. Leslie Hotson notices that the impress of the seal Munday used on his will was "the pelican in her piety" (*Notes and Queries* 204 [1959]: 4).

[52] "The Contextualization of Source Material: The Play Within the Play in *Sir Thomas More*," *Le Forme del Teatro* 3 (1984): 71–74.

[53] *On the Literary Genetics of Shakspere's Plays: 1592–1594* (Urbana: Univ. of Illinois Press, 1959), 44–45; see what appears to be a second thought on 517. The possibility of traces of Munday is discussed in Appendix D.

[54] Jenkins seems puzzled by the omission, in *Henry Chettle*, 6–7. On the topical allusions in *Catharos*, see Alice Walker, *Review of English Studies* 8 (1932): 266–67; Richard Helgerson, *The Elizabethan Prodigals* (Berkeley: Univ. of California Press, 1976), chap. 6.

because he was otherwise uneducated. Compositors must have good memories, at least short term, in order to hold a line of words in mind while reaching for and placing type. Chettle may have been able, up to a point, to imitate Greene's style. He mimicked the voices of five ghosts in *Kind-Heart's Dream*, one of whom was Greene, and, of course, did voices in writing plays. Peter Blayney thinks he detects in *Kind-Heart's* echoes of words, largely in the form of clusters, from the 148-line Shakespeare section of *More* (Hand D), echoes working at a "less-than-conscious level." That Shakespeare passage in *More*, Scott McMillin says, must have insinuated its "word into the book and volume of Henry Chettle's brain."[55] "Nothing," Chettle tells us in his preface to *Kind-Heart's*, "can be said, that hath not been before said." This comment would not appear to be so utterly gratuitous if Chettle is trying through it to explain and justify his attribution to Greene of a book which he himself wrote, a book made up out of words and phrases from, and modeled on the arrangement of, works by Greene. Notice the way the preface opens: "It hath beene a custome Gentle men (in my mind commendable) among former Authors (whose workes are not lesse beautified with eloquente phrase, than garnished with excellent example)...." The words *beautified* and *garnished* recall the attack on Shakespeare, illustrating his special talent.

The dispute that brought Danter and Chettle before the Stationers' court on 5 March 1593, and ("in lyke sort") on that same day Danter and Burby, printer and publisher, respectively, of *The Repentance*, has never been explained.[56] It may have been over rights to or profits from these two books. It is, however, possible that the three were formally enjoined on this occasion from continuing to misrepresent these two books. It seems odd that no evidence remains of other editions of *Groatsworth* for four years or any of *The Repentance* ever after—considering that there were at least six of *Quip* in 1592 and in the same year eight, altogether, of the first three cony-catching pam-

[55] Blayney, "*The Booke of Sir Thomas Moore* Re-Examined," 181–91. Richard Proudfoot thinks Blayney attaches too much weight to these "reminiscences," in *Shakespeare Survey* 26 (1973): 183; and Gary Taylor, after a full analysis, is unconvinced of real "links" between the two texts, in "The Date and Auspices of the Additions to *Sir Thomas More*," *Shakespeare and "Sir Thomas More*," 114–18. John Jowett, in "Henry Chettle and the Original Text of *Sir Thomas More*," ibid., 135, found one of the Blayney parallels convincing, which might be enough. The matter may not admit of settlement. McMillin, *Elizabethan Theatre and "The Book of Sir Thomas More*," 147.

[56] W. W. Greg and E. Boswell, *Records of the Court of the Stationers' Company* (London: Bibliographical Society, 1930), 46.

phlets. Finally, since the second half, the part which seems the more susceptible to "editing," was printed in Danter's shop, where, we presume, Chettle came and went, some contributions could have been made to that half while printing was underway. The circumstances involving these individuals do not provide strong evidence one way or the other, but they do suggest a climate in which forgery or unacknowledged collaboration could take place.

Still other external evidence might implicate Chettle. First, if Chettle got the manuscript immediately after 3 September, we may wonder why, when haste was all important, it took until its registration on 20 September merely to copy it over. A period of over two weeks suggests something more than transcription, if something less than full composition. We may wonder, too, why Burby's shorter *Repentance*, entered on 6 October, took even longer. Second, *Groatsworth* was entered to Wright "uppon the perill of *Henrye Chettle*."[57] Sanders takes this "peculiar wording" to indicate that Wright, having foreseen trouble with the content and wanting to free himself, held the true author, Chettle, responsible for its content. In Jenkins' view the entry suggests no more than Wright's intent to safeguard himself in the only way he could, using someone alive, since he could see that the manuscript contained potentially troublesome material.[58] The entry cannot in itself be taken as *proof* that Wright knew or suspected that Chettle had written some or all of it. Nevertheless, it is just what Wright would demand if he knew Chettle wrote it. W. A. Jackson found both early entries of *Groatsworth* "baffling," the second because it shows no clear transfer of ownership from Wright. On 20 October 1596 Thomas Creede and Richard Olive "Entred for Richard Oliffes Copie Greenes *groates of witt* printed by John Danter." The two books for which there were also transfers of ownership that day, one of which is *Kind-Heart's*, are indeed listed as Wright's. Wright either did not own *Groatsworth* or, keeping his distance, wanted to give that impression.[59] Third, Wright, who in his epistle to *Groatsworth* describes it as Greene's "last," seems not to have known that two other books already with printers (*Repentance* and *Greene's Vision*) would describe themselves in the same way. If Chettle had known of either book, he would surely have adjusted Wright's epistle. That neither Wright nor Chettle seems aware of the existence of *The Repentance*,

---

[57] *Transcript*, ed. Arber, 2:620. The one similar entry, which grants permission to print to Richard Jones "of his own perill" (2:428), involves, as Sanders judged it ("Greene and His 'Editors,'" 396 n.), a question of ownership.

[58] Sanders, "Greene and His 'Editors,'" 395–96; Jenkins, "Authenticity," 32.

[59] *Pforzheimer Catalogue*, 2:415–16; *Transcript*, ed. Arber, 3:72.

and there is absolutely no hint of it in *Groatsworth* or no hint of *Groatsworth* in it, weakens the credibility of both books as Greene's deathbed work. Finally, the name of neither printer appears as part of the imprint, and the Wolfe device on the title page (though it looks like a wolf-mask) was one rarely used (it is not listed in McKerrow's book of devices).

∽

What is the evidence, external to the text, for Greene's authorship beyond Chettle's assertion in his preface? He may have been, as the epistle to *Groatsworth* has it, "able inough to write" some or all, despite his sickness, though, unless doubts were anticipated in the matter, such would seem to go without saying. Greene was ill for "about a moneths space," Burby reports in *The Repentance*, but he could walk "to his chaire and backe again [as late as] the night before he departed."[60] But Burby's word may not be trustworthy, since, as publisher of *Repentance* and perhaps aware of suspicions about *Groatsworth*, he needs us to believe Greene could have worked on. Greene wrote quickly, we know from Nashe, a talent that had earned him good money: "In a night and a day would he have yarkt up a Pamphlet," and printers were anxious to "pay him deare for the very dregs of his wit."[61] Moreover, we can believe Greene understood as well as Chettle the value of his name and, sick and burdened with a large entourage, could more than match Chettle for need.

One possibility is that he had on hand material composed some time before and put aside, apparently a practice with him. *Philomela*, entered on 1 July 1592, was "writen long since and kept charily," as "scollers treasurs be, in loose papers."[62] *Greene's Vision*, for which our earliest edition is late in 1592, must have been written in 1590. *Farewell to Folly*, for which our earliest edition is 1591, was entered on 11 June 1587. *Opharion*, entered on 9 January 1590, he mentioned over a year before, in the preface to *Perimedes*. "Cuthbert Connycatcher" asking Greene why he wrote of petty criminals and not of

---

[60] Ed. Harrison, 31–32. The account of his illness, by Burby presumably, suggests that he died of dropsy, a morbid condition characterized by the accumulation of watery fluid in the serous cavities or the connective tissue of the body (ascites), itself caused by a form of liver disease, perhaps in consequence of too much alcohol in general, probably not from that fatal banquet of rhenish wine and pickled herring. Cf. *Groatsworth*, 766–67: "his immeasurable drinking had made him the perfect Image of the dropsie." On Falstaff's death from a similar disorder, see Henry D. Janowitz, M.D., in *Cahiers Élizabéthain* 33 (1988): 53–55.

[61] *Nashe*, ed. McKerrow, 1:287.

[62] *Works*, ed. Grosart, 11:109.

usurers in *The Defence of Cony-Catching*, entered 21 April 1592, may (if the book is by Greene, as some think) constitute an advertisement for the Roberto story of *Groatsworth* already in hand or mind, with its old usurer Gorinius. *The Repentance* may be be made up out of material adapted from that announced repentance volume. "[M]any papers," Chettle says in that preface, he left "in sundry Booke sellers hands."

Printed comments of three contemporaries may bear on the question. First, B. R., who must be Barnabe Riche, in *Greene's News Both from Heaven and Hell*, entered on 3 February 1593, has Greene's ghost identify *Groatsworth* as "one other of my bookes."[63] Riche, who had just moved to London from Ireland in the summer, claims he never met Greene. Second, R. B., probably Richard Barnfield, in a sonnet in defense of Greene in *Greene's Funerals*, entered 1 February 1594 but probably written soon after Greene's death, seems to repeat the "beautified with our feathers" charge of the letter to the playwrights:

> Greene, *gave the ground, to all that wrote upon him.*
> *Nay more[,] the men, that so Eclipst his fame:*
> *Purloynde his Plumes, can they deny the same?*

But here, even if this passage does recall the letter, which has been questioned, it does not follow that Barnfield thought Greene had written *Groatsworth*.[64] Barnfield, who turned eighteen in the summer of 1592, may have written it before *Groatsworth* was out, relying on rumors, ones Chettle would also know. Third, Harvey takes Nashe to task for being *"Greenes advocate"* as follows: "He may declare his deere affection to his Paramour: or his pure honestye to the world; or his constant zeale to play the Divels Oratour: but noe Apology of Greene, like *Greenes Grotes-worth of witt*: and when Nash will indeede accomplish a worke of Supererogation, let him publish, Nashes *Penniworth of Discretion*."[65] *Apology of* probably means *apology for* or *defense of*. Harvey's main point seems to be that Nashe's defense of

---

[63] Ed. McKerrow, 11. See my "Barnaby Riche and Robert Greene: Beast Fables and Ireland," *Éire-Ireland* 25 (1990): 106–13.

[64] Ed. McKerrow, 81. On Warren B. Austin's view, in *Shakespeare Quarterly* 6 (1950): 374–80, that the sonnet does not allude to *Groatsworth*, see the discussion, below, in Appendix G.

[65] *Pierces Supererogation*, 1593, STC 12903, E2ʳ; *Works*, ed. Grosart, 2:75. Note also John Fletcher in verses prefatory to Jonson's *Catiline* (1611): critics with bad taste will call "for mad *Pasquill*, / Or *Greene*'s dear *Groatsworth*, or *Tom Coryate*" (*Jonson*, ed. C. H. Herford, Percy and Evelyn Simpson [Oxford: Clarendon Press, 1952], 11:325).

Greene is not ingenuous, as *Groatsworth* is, which condemns more than it defends. It need not imply that Greene wrote it.

ॐ

We turn now to the content and style of *Groatsworth*, to identify its sources and to elicit what we can as evidence for authorship. Whether by Greene or not, in certain obvious ways *Groatsworth* appears to be by him. Its motifs and method seem to be his, and it can be closely tied to several works by or related to him. Within the last two years Greene had made repentance his literary theme and used it, as here, with the prodigal son motif. *Groatsworth* reflects his tendencies to model fiction after features of his own life and to appropriate matter he, or others, had already used. Typically, it does not sustain its strong, initial narrative, but, especially after the middle, seems padded, with its list of precepts, two letters, and two poems. And it contains some euphuisms, which had been, at least early on, a trick of Greene's style.[66] An imitator might have felt obliged to use some. They disappear after the middle of the book.

Of greater interest are links with four specific works, three by Greene. *Groatsworth* bears a striking resemblance to the two parts of *Greene's Never Too Late*, the second of which is titled *Francesco's Fortunes*, both unregistered but probably published in 1590. In the first part, the protagonist, Francesco, has a name which, like Roberto's, is a shadow, "for that the Gentleman is yet living," and his story takes place in England. In "the chief city of that Iland," he succumbs, like Roberto's brother Lucanio, to the seduction of a courtesan, and is cast out when his money is wasted. This Francesco, like Roberto, is "a Scholler, and nurst up in the Universities" and has a wife not living with him. There are numerous, obvious lexical parallels—"beautifie," "famoused," "fetching the compasse," "extremitie(s)" (3), among others—and parallel images, especially in descriptions of the courtesan and her wiles—Syrens (3), Calipso, Circes (4), Medusa, and "painted sepulchers." As in *Groatsworth*, hair is like "amber tramells," eyes like basilisks' (2), eyes and heart are of adamant (3), and so on. In *Groatsworth* Lamilia "tainted her cheekes with a vermilion blush" (line 356); in *Never* Infida is presented as "dying her face with a Vermillion blush," and Francesco's song has "Hir face . . . / All tainted through with bright Vermillion staines." And *Never's*

---

[66] Nashe, with exaggeration, identified euphuism with Greene; *Nashe*, 1:319, 3:132.

account of Francesco's elopement has the same realistic flavor found in Roberto's tale of the slandered bridegroom.[67]

In the sequel, Francesco, like Roberto, turns in his poverty to playwriting and becomes a sudden success. A digression on plays and playmakers, like the famous letter to the playwrights, attacks players for their greed and insolence and employs a fable of the crow (which begins): "why *Roscius*, art thou proud with *Esops* Crow, being pranct with the glorie of others feathers?" The lexical parallels occur— "beautified," "famozed," "momentarie" (2), "secretarie" (2), "extremitie" (4), among others—and the same comparisons for women— Syrens, Calipsos (2), Circe, hyena, basilisks, "amber tresses," "tramels of her haire," "hearts like adamants" (3), and so on. The whole is padded with letters, poems, and precepts.[68]

Greene's Mourning Garment, entered 2 November 1590, uses the prodigal son motif, though its structure and character conform closely to the biblical account. Unlike *Groatsworth*, *Garment* has a kindly father, a prodigal younger brother, who learns "too late repentance, . . . having bought witte at too deare a rate," and a jealous elder brother. In *Groatsworth* and *Garment* courtesans entertain the prodigals in very similar ways, cheating them at dice and rejecting them when they have wasted their wealth. Philador saves a would-be suicide from despair in the same way the Player-Patron in *Groatsworth* saves Roberto. There are, again, the lexical parallels—"beautified," "famozed" (2), "momentany-ary" (3), "Secretary," "extremity" (7), among others—and the same comparisons for the courtesans—Syrens (10), Calipsos (2), Circe (5), hyena (2), basilisk (2), Scilla, "painted sepulchres," women who catch men in the "tramels of [their] locks" (*tramels* occurs twice), who are "Adamants that drawe," have "faces like Adamants" (*adamants* occurs 4 times), and so on. Rosamond, a courtesan, is described as "dying all her face with a vermillion blush." There are assorted poems, a list of precepts, and a repentance theme that Greene announces in the dedication as his new mood and insists on throughout.[69]

Groatsworth clearly repeats attitudes and phrases that appear in Nashe's preface to Greene's *Menaphon*, entered in August 1589. It is the poets, Nashe says, including among them George Peele, as does

---

[67] That quoted is from, ed. Grosart, 8:33, 66, 64, 28, 33, 37, 40, 42, 60, 107, 93, 71, 93.

[68] That quoted is from, ed. Grosart, 8:132, 121, 125, 222, 168, 174, 128, 129, 134, 185, 123, 178, 135, 182, 205.

[69] That quoted is from, ed. Grosart, 9:186, 130, 147, 174, 157, 194, 195, 138, 182, 184, 186, 187, 188, 192, 210, 190, 149, 128, 138, 207 131, 190, 155. The brothel scene occurs at 176–86. The commentary makes at least 12 other references to *Never*, 10 to *Francisco's*, and 18 to *Garment*.

Groatsworth, who have brought to the actors the fame and fortune which serves as the basis for their new-found pride:

Sundry other sweete Gentlemen I doe know, that have vaunted their pennes in private devices, and tricked up a company of taffaty fooles with their feathers, whose beauty if our Poets had not peecte with the supply of their periwigs, they might have antickt it untill this time up and downe the Countrey with the King of Fairies, and dined every day at the pease porredge ordinary with *Delfrigus*.

But *Tolossa* hath forgotten that it was sometime sacked, and beggars that ever they carried their fardels on footback. . . .[70]

From this account came the shape and some of the details for the Player-Patron's career in *Groatsworth*. His own style being now out of fashion, he turns to scholars like Roberto, through whom he has grown wealthy. "[M]en of my profession," he says, "gette by schollers their whole living. . . . What though the world once went hard with me, when I was faine to carry my playing Fardle a footebacke, . . . it is otherwise now . . . why, I am as famous for Delphrigus, and the King of Fairies, as ever as any of my time. . . ." (lines 653–69). This preface must be a primary source for the attack on Shakespeare. Nashe has actors who would "embowell the cloudes in a speech of comparison," playwrights who "thinke to out-brave better pennes with the swelling bumbast of bragging blanke verse," and pamphleteers who vaunt "*Ovids* and *Plutarchs* plumes as theyr owne."[71] From these lines, in part, comes the following: "Yes trust them not: for there is an upstart Crow, beautified with our feathers, that with his *Tygers hart wrapt in a Players hyde*, supposes he is as well able to bombast out a blanke verse as the best of you: and beeing an absolute *Johannes fac totum*, is in his owne conceit the onely Shake-scene in a countrey" (lines 938–43).

Warren Austin's explanation for some of these connections is quite plausible: Chettle deliberately patterned his forgery on Greene episodes (the brothel episodes in particular) and passages in order to make it appear to be Greene's, and produced thereby, in places, nothing more than *pastiches* of Greene. Chettle's procedure, he says, accounts for a slight anomaly turned up by his computer study. In *Groatsworth* a number of "Greene-favored words," occurring 22 times altogether, have a frequency rate twice that in Chettle, though still

---

[70] *Nashe*, 3:323–24.
[71] *Nashe*, 3:311–12.

only one-fourth what we would expect if *Groatsworth* were Greene's. Seven of these words appearing both in the source episodes and in their *Groatsworth* counterparts do not appear at all in the Chettle corpus. Austin is certainly justified in seeing that the dependency here is not that often described as Greene's "self-plagiarism."[72] *Groatsworth* echoes (paraphrases) Greene; it rarely repeats or quotes at length in the way we might expect from Greene's earlier practice. We could·not from it produce the kind of repetitions Gordon Coggins gives in his study of Greene, where some entries approach the "sixe lines at a clap" that Nashe complained someone pilfered from him.[73] *Groatsworth* does suggest the books of 1590, as my commentary shows, in diction, which includes some phrasing, in situation, and in its stock of allusions and proverbs, a resemblance which could easily be calculated by a competent imitator. But *Groatsworth*'s style in general is not especially distinctive, certainly not, despite a number of obvious links, distinctively Greene's. Neither Sanders nor Pruvost, in the days before the computer, thought it possible to make an attribution on stylistic grounds.[74]

Austin argues that Chettle's verbal habits predominate even while "he imitated Greene's typical content, general style, and prominent mannerisms," and adopted some of his words. His study "resoundingly confirms the hypothesis that the book is a literary forgery."[75] Austin contrasts the styles of the two authors in ten classes of variables: favored words, high-frequency words, uncommon words, prefixes, suffixes, reflexive pronouns, gerund plurals, compound words, parentheses, and word-order inversion. In every one of these classes, presented through tables that give occurrences per 1000 words, the frequency appears to be more compatible with Chettle's style than with Greene's, revealing, in great detail, linguistic fingerprints that are difficult to ignore. The forgery is total, he thinks. Even the 1127-word letter to the playwrights, to which he gives special

---

[72] "Greene's Attack on Shakespeare: A Posthumous Hoax," *Shakespeare Newsletter* 16 (Sept. 1966): 30; "Technique of the Chettle-Greene Forgery," ibid., 20 (Dec. 1970): 43; *Computer-Aided Technique*, 4.

[73] "Greene's Repetitions as Solutions to Textual Problems: A Catalogue of Repetitions," *Analytical & Enumerative Bibliography* 5 (1981): 3–15; *Nashe*, 3:132.

[74] "Greene and His 'Editors,'" 399; *Robert Greene*, 512. S. Schoenbaum found C. M. Ingleby's reaction to Collier's suggestion of a Chettle forgery in the margin of the Folger copy of J. O. Halliwell-Phillipps' *Life* (1848, p. 143): "An absurd conjecture. Greene's work is full of genius, whereas Chettle was a poor stick, & could hardly write English" (in *William Shakespeare: A Documentary Life*, 118 n.).

[75] "Technique," 43; *Computer-Aided Technique*, 78.

treatment, can be shown, "somewhat surprisingly" because of its brevity, to be Chettle's. For anyone who takes the trouble to secure a copy of the study, grasp its method, and interpret its 46 tables, the evidence in thousands of pieces of stylistic data, so arranged, does point to Chettle. (Austin's conclusions are reprinted in Appendix B.) It also allows for some questions.

Austin's Greene data base for considering the 10,999-word *Groatsworth* contains 104,596 words from five prose works of mixed genres published in the last two years of his career. Reviewers wanted the base to be a larger fraction of the 700,000-word corpus, to be more nearly uniform in genre, and to cover a larger time period.[76] *Groatsworth* itself is rather short. The Chettle base is of necessity quite meager, perhaps too meager: the 43,190 words of his acknowledged prose (excluding certain epistles used as controls). It is also mixed in genre and ranges in publication date from 1592 to 1603. Moreover, no single category deals with large quantities of evidence. Thus the 3.82 instances per 1000 of *-self* words in *Groatsworth* is judged to be closer to the 3.79 of Chettle than to the 2.32 of Greene. But one may ask, with Thomas W. Cobb, if this is "a truly distinctive stylistic difference." And, to take a second example Cobb discusses, while the 4 gerund plurals in *Groatsworth*, twice the 2 in the Greene corpus, are indeed closer to the 14 in the smaller Chettle corpus, 4 is not much to go on.[77] Yet when enough data such as these accumulate, the whole gathers weight.

Greene never uses any of the combinative conjunctive-adverb forms in *-ever* (*however, whatever,* etc.), but always the *-soever* forms, whereas the author of *Groatsworth* prefers the *-ever* forms more than three-fourths of the time (10 to 2), which approaches Chettle's preference (22 to 7), producing "the strongest single piece of lexical

---

[76] Reviewers were unduly hard on Austin. See Thomas M. Pearce (with Austin's response), *Shakespeare Newsletter* 21 (Feb. 1971): 4; T. R. Waldo, *Computers and the Humanities* 7 (1972): 109–10; R. L. Widmann, *Shakespeare Quarterly* 23 (1972): 214–15; Richard Proudfoot, *Shakespeare Survey* 26 (1973): 182–83. The fullest response, which rejects Austin's conclusion, is Thomas W. Cobb, "A Critical Edition of Robert Greene's *Groatsworth of Wit,*" unpubl. Ph.D. diss., Yale Univ., 1977, cxxxi–iv, cccix–xxiii. Barbara Kreifelts, in her 1972 Cologne diss., *Eine statistische Stilanalyse* (129 pp.), which finds Chettle the likely author, considers such criteria as relative frequency and distance apart of the same words or words of the same length, length of sentences, quotient of repetition, and occurrence of high-frequency and once-used words. Her work is abstracted in *Shakespeare Newsletter* 26 (Dec. 1974): 49, and in Werner Habicht, ed., *English and American Studies in German. Summaries of Theses and Monographs.* A Supplement to *Anglia,* 1972 (Tübingen: Max Niemeyer, 1973), 53–54.

[77] "Critical Edition," cli–ii.

evidence."[78] *Groatsworth* has 9 *O*s (and no *Oh*s), which Chettle elsewhere favors strongly (19 to 1) and Greene does not (13 to 44). The frequency of parentheses in *Groatsworth* per 1000 words at 4.81 corresponds closely to Chettle's (4.69), not Greene's (1.34). The percentage of *yes* among *yes* and *you*s is 18.7 for *Groatsworth*, closer to Chettle's 38.3 than to Greene's 0.5.[79] Cobb thinks that editing, a deep editing we might say, when Chettle "writ it over," could account for these features and still allow him, under threatening circumstances, to deny authorship in sweeping terms.[80] But the evidence, Austin asserts, is "too thoroughly intrinsic to have been produced by editorial revision."[81] Austin's work does not settle the matter, but it makes impossible an outright dismissal of the idea of a substantial role for Chettle, especially since much of the external evidence supports such a conclusion. All questions of attribution may one day be settled by statistical analysis (stylometry). Austin has brought that day closer.

Certain other features of the text (tone, structure, and treatment of the prodigal son motif), it is true, have given some the impression that it is Greene's. Readers can judge for themselves. My own impression is that this kind of evidence leads to no conclusion either way. The success of the book as an apparent expression of a Greene deathbed repentance may be due to the cleverness of the forger.

Some have heard an authenticity in the voice, a private pain breaking through the public form. Nicholas Storojenko would "fearlessly believe [Greene] when he speaks of the anguish of his soul and the sincerity of his repentance."[82] J. A. Symonds thought "the accent of remorse . . . too sincere and strongly marked [in these last works] to justify a suspicion of deliberate fiction."[83] As for the famous letter, there has been almost unanimous agreement that its bitterness is genuine, its "earnestness," as Dyce put it, "scarcely consistent with

---

[78] *Computer-Aided Technique*, 23.

[79] Austin cites Cyrus Hoy, *Studies in Bibliography* 8 (1961): 142, 138, to show the value of *ye-you* in distinguishing between authors. Jowett ("Henry Chettle," 140–41) gives some weight to this apparent preference in helping determine Chettle's share of *More*, but wonders if the tone of the context might matter, *ye* being "more informal, idiomatic or intimate."

[80] "Critical Edition," cxxxv. Pierce, *Shakespeare Newsletter* 21 (Feb. 1971): 4, takes this view also.

[81] *Shakespeare Newsletter* 21 (Feb. 1971): 4. From an Austin transcript, *Shakespeare Newsletter* 16 (Sept. 1966): 29–30, summarizes arguments that may turn up a second book.

[82] In Grosart, ed., *Works*, 1:64.

[83] *Shakspere's Predecessors*, 435.

forgery."[84] "Sincerity and reality," for A. B. Grosart, "pulsate in every word of these ultimate utterances."[85] Those who hear real remorse and bitterness throughout the last pages will have little trouble assigning the whole to Greene. But there are those who may hear, instead, something studied, overly self-conscious and literary. It may be Greene's, of course, even if it strikes us as out-and-out claptrap. His attitude elsewhere, in works unquestionably his, raises doubts, about, for examples, the sincerity of his program for exposing cony-catchers, the motive for which some judge to have been largely mercenary, or the sincerity of his earlier spasms of remorse, the books of 1590, which some have thought had solely to do with fashion. Greg had "a strong suspicion that Greene . . . adopted the machinery of repentance by way of explaining and advertising a change of style," a view J. C. Jordan inclined to accept.[86] "The more one knows of him," Jordan concluded, "the less one finds that is sincere, that comes from the depth of character, from bigness of attitude toward life"; and yet Jordan got "an impression of greater sincerity" from the last pages of *Groatsworth* and from *Repentance*.[87] This difference Richard Helgerson also felt: "His literary repentance was the child of fashion, and his personal repentance was the child of God."[88] One passage might be something of a test: "Blacke is the remembrance of my blacke workes, blacker than night, blacker than death, blacker than hell" (lines 829–31). Cobb takes it both ways: "the seeming exaggeration [here is] both typical of Elizabethan repentance literature and at the same time not at all incompatible with deeply felt sincerity."[89]

The very features of *Groatsworth* which appear suspicious—its discontinuities—have been taken as testimonials to its authenticity. Thus it was for Pruvost: "Nous la trouvons encore, et de façon plus décisive, dans le fait qu'à mesure que l'on avance dans sa lecture on semble assister, d'étape en étape, aux progrès de l'inquiétude dans l'esprit du malade."[90] That shift in point of view from third to first person which clinches the identification between the prodigal and a Greene infamous for his prodigality is called by Helgerson "one of the

---

[84] Ed., *Works of William Shakespeare* (London, 1857), 1:xliv, n.; also in *Works of Christopher Marlowe* (1850; repr. London, 1858), xxxi.

[85] Ed., *Works*, 1:xii.

[86] *Modern Language Review* 1 (1906): 241; Jordan, *Robert Greene*, 70.

[87] *Robert Greene*, 95, 71.

[88] *Elizabethan Prodigals*, 102.

[89] "Critical Edition," cxcii.

[90] *Robert Greene*, 513.

most remarkable passages in sixteenth-century fiction."[91] To some it may seem desperately natural. Only a writer in deep trouble, feeling the pressure of the personal on the story, could have imagined it; only someone with Greene's literary instincts could have appreciated its bold rightness. Even before the break, in the tightening identity between the two, the fictional disguise seems to give way, unable to contain and otherwise ease real anxieties.

Distortions in the *Groatsworth*'s prodigal son story have also suggested an engagement that could have been Greene's. After a thorough comparison with examples of the story which precede it, by Greene and others, Cobb declares it "as pessimistic a version of the parable as had perhaps ever appeared." Its assessment of human worth is negative, he finds, its appraisal of the dealings of the world cynical, its every character "the most distressing and cynical portrayal of human nature possible." This "odd treatment" Cobb attributes to "the dominating autobiographical relevancies and utterances." The father, who normally stands for positive values in the story, is a vicious usurer, an alteration which might suggest Greene, for whom masculine authorities (fathers, husbands, elders, rulers) are usually mean spirited. The elder brother, who in the original develops unacceptable but justifiable hostilities toward the penitent prodigal, is made the center of the story, the stand-in for Greene, a shift which allows for the exploitation of ambivalences Greene may have felt. The father ridicules Roberto's high principles and disinherits him (but for an old groat). And when the father dies, Roberto, thus provoked, in a way we would not have expected, takes revenge against his brother, who loses all and virtually disappears from the story. Roberto, now become the prodigal, commits himself to the vices of the city after turning in his need, and thereby abusing his talents, to playwriting (the symbolic equivalent of swineherding), a development with no parallel in contemporary versions of the story.[92]

Throughout the book, Roberto is presented as both victim and sinner, embittered because of genuine grievances (abused and disinherited by the father, mistreated by the players, abandoned by friends), penitent for obvious sins, anxious for forgiveness and, finally, for salvation, and yet desperate of any expectation. Since the father is

---

[91] *Elizabethan Prodigals*, 80.

[92] Cobb, "Critical Edition," cc–cccviii. Cobb's discussion is excellent; see also those by Jordan, *Robert Greene*, chap. 3, and Helgerson, *Elizabethan Prodigals*, chap. 5. Helgerson's book treats the way creative writers of the period, especially the University Wits, identified with the prodigal son in their works and felt this identification in their lives. Quotations are from Cobb, ccxci, cclxxxviii–iv, ccxcii.

made to die early on, the reconciliation and forgiveness of the classical parable become impossible, in what is perhaps a radical, Calvinis-
tic version, and the story therefore unresolvable. This impasse allows
for a break from narrative into confessional mode, where supplication
is possible. That it begins in self-justification and ends in near despair
may suggest to some how the man who "replaced Euphues as the
most popular representative" of the prodigal son type (Helgerson)
actually confronted sickness and death.[93] Be that as it may, one is
permitted to wonder if Greene would write a story so unlike, in its
cynicism, anything he had written before, and if he would present so
cruel a portrait of someone (Gorinius) who stands for his father,
whatever their relationship had been. With a few superficial changes
(the names and the single reference to his marriage) up to the middle
of the book, the Roberto story and its sentiments would better reflect
what we know of the life of Lodge, who was at least as notorious in
London as Greene for a prodigal.[94]

   Though in the main a forgery, in my judgment, the book may
contain some matter by Greene and/or someone else and thus be, in
a minor way, a collaboration. What struck Jenkins about Chettle's
career as a hackwriter with Henslowe, besides his penury, was his
remarkable ability to adapt and alter other men's work according to
the needs of the moment, and the speed with which he could do
so.[95] The evidence for forgery is not, and can never be, conclusive.
That some part, even if minor, may be by Greene ought to be acknowledged in the book's designation, as long as scholars understand
the nature and strength of the case for Chettle. Only with the famous
letter to the playwrights will an adjustment for the probability of
forgery be difficult. The caretakers of the story of Shakespeare will
want to go on hearing the voice of someone who counted, a major
playwright displaced by Shakespeare's arrival, who understood completely and suffered personally from what it meant. We cannot be
certain whose views we get. Everything about Chettle suggests that he
repeats what is current. It is highly improbable that he would present
attitudes toward Marlowe and Shakespeare which were not, or were
not widely thought to be, Greene's. That we learn from the letter
something about Shakespeare, of the success of his advent in the envy
it generated, is what matters most, and we are grateful for the apology

---

[93] Helgerson, 79, who has Greene, in explaining his own repentances, "move
toward radical Protestantism" (102).
[94] See, above, note 23.
[95] See *Henry Chettle*, 19ff.

the letter provoked from Chettle. Jenkins was also impressed with Chettle's "innate literary ability."[96]

As for its date, therefore, the book took on final form between 3 and 20 September, some of the material having been written already. The primary tasks must have been, first, shaping the end of the Roberto story so as to make it conform to known events of Greene's life (mentioning the cony-catching pamphlets, incorporating the material from Harvey), second, writing several of the fragments, including the epistle and letter to his wife, and finally, providing the joinery, in the last quarter, for these fragments. "*Lamilias Fable*" and "*Robertoes Tale*," two minor pieces in modes popular in 1591–1592 (beast fable, realistic tale), could have been on hand or already attached to the Roberto story; neither is much relevant or even interesting where it occurs in the book. Most of the Roberto narrative, judging by the way its tone differs from that of the end of the book, had to have been written before Greene's death.[97]

---

[96] *Henry Chettle*, 22.

[97] Cobb alone sees no incongruity between the Roberto story and the remainder of the book. He finds a consistency in the meanness or cruelty of the piece, in its grim philosophy, its sardonic humor. For G. B. Harrison "the discreditable adventures of Roberto are related with a zest which suggests that the author was amused rather than stricken to heart" (*Shakespeare's Fellows* [London: John Lane, 1923], 63).

Text

Early Editions

The six early editions are described in detail and accurately, with the title page of each edition reproduced in microfiche, by A. F. Allison, in *Robert Greene, 1558–1592: A Bibliographical Catalogue of the Early Editions in English (to 1640)* (Folkestone, Kent: Dawson, 1975). University Microfilm (Ann Arbor) has available and has distributed to principal research libraries copies of each edition. Scolar Press (Menston, Yorks., 1969) has a facsimile of Q1 (British Library). The title page of Q1 (Folger) is reproduced here as frontispiece.

1592 (Q1) Ent. S. R., 20 September 1592. STC 12245
John Wolfe printed sheets A–C, John Danter sheets D–F; see Sidney Thomas, *Studies in Bibliography* 19 (1966): 196–97.

Copies: (* = examined; both copies collated. No apparent press variants.) *Folger (Fenn-Frere-White) (–A1). Copy-text / *British Library (+A1) (C.57.b.42) (purchased from a provincial bookseller in 1909) (U. M. I., Reel 838).

1596 (Q2) STC 12246
Copies: *Folger (some of the text of F1, and possibly other leaves, appears to be in facs.) / *Ransom, U. of Texas (Wrangham-Britwell-Pforzheimer) / *Huntington (61157; Jolley-Corser-Huth) (U. M. I., Reel 385). Copy collated.

1617 (Q3) STC 12247
Beginning with this edition a different preliminary dedication replaces the original two and the poem "Greenes Epitaph" is added at the end (both given in Appendix A). Both are signed "I. H.," presumably

John Hind or Hynd (attr. to him in the Huth Catalogue, [1880], 2:624), a writer who imitated Greene. The old BM Catalogue ([1946], 24:88) suggests Jasper Heywood.

Copies: *Folger₁ (G4 mended, with some of text supplied in facs.). Copy collated / *Folger₂ (F. Locker-Lampson) (E4–G4 lacking, supplied in MS) / *British Library (95.b.20(5)) / *Bodleian (Wood 614/9) (U. M. I., Reel 1519) / *Ransom, University of Texas (Brereton-Dysart-Ham House-Pforzheimer) / Chapin, Williams College (Halliwell-Huth-Levy) / Rosenbach (Corser-White) / Österreichische Nationalbibliothek, Vienna / John Wolfson, New York City (imperfect).

1621 (Q4)   **STC 12248**
Copies: *Folger₁ (–F4) (Marsh-Harmsworth) / *Folger₂ (–F4) (Warwick Castle) / *Folger₃ (fragment, E4 only) (Halliwell-Phillipps copy?) / *British Library (C.40.d.41) (title mounted, missing "GREENES," E4 cropped, wants all after E4) / *Victoria and Albert (Dyce Collection, D.25.c.4y) (+F4, cropped) / *Bodleian (4⁰.C110 Th./2) (–F4) / *Trinity College, Cambridge (S.36⁰) (–F4) (Capell) / *Huntington (–F4) (U. M. I., Reel 1380). Copy collated /Beinecke, Yale U. / Hickmott, Dartmouth College (–F4) (Cardiff).

1629 (Q5)   **STC 12249**
Copies: *Bodleian (Malone 572/9) (–A1, F4) / *Huntington (Allison: +A1, F4) (Gardner-Britwell) (U. M. I., Reel 1380). Copy collated / Boston Public Library.

1637 (Q6)   **STC 12250**
Page-for-page reprint of Q5. Allison wonders if R. Hearne is the printer; K. Pantzer suggests R. Hodgkinson (New *STC* 1:537).

Copies: *Folger (–A1, +F4?) (Halliwell-Phillipps-Maidment). Copy collated / *British Library (95.b.16) (–A1, F4) / *Bodleian (Douce G254) (–A1, F4) (U. M. I., Reel 1519) / *Worcester College, Oxford (two copies, both –A1, F4) / *Trinity College, Cambridge (Capell Q.14) (–A1, F4) / *Pierpont Morgan (–A1, F4) (Utterson-Irwin) / Beinecke, Yale U. (–A1, F4) / Meisei U., Tokyo (–A1, apparently +F4) (Sion College) / Robert H. Taylor, Princeton U.

Early Publication History

The first transfer of rights to *Groatsworth*, like the original entry of 20 September 1592 (Arber, 2:620) with its "vppon the perill of *Henrye Chettle*," is somewhat puzzling, "baffling," to W. A. Jackson, *Pforzheimer Catalogue*, 2:415–16. The Register for 20 October 1596 has the following: "Entred for *Richard Oliffes* Copie GREENES *groates of witt* printed by *John Danter*. And *Thomas creede* from tyme to tyme to print this book for *Richard Oliff*" (3:72). The two other items with which it appears, *Kind-Heart's Dream* being one, are clearly transferred to Creede from William Wright, the man who entered the first edition. Wright either did not own it or else did not want to acknowledge ownership. Creede printed it for Olive in 1596 (Q2). From his widow Elizabeth Olive it passed on 6 November 1615 to Phillip Knight (3:575), and from Knight to Henry Bell on 5 January 1616 (3:581), for whom it was printed by Barnard Alsop in 1617 (Q3), by Nicholas Oakes in 1621 (Q4), by John Haviland in 1629 (Q5), and, when Bell is joined by his brother Moses, by a printer not identified in 1637 (Q6). Ownership passed from the Bells to Haviland and John Wright on 4 September 1638 (4:434). Representatives from some early editions may not survive. Each surviving edition but one (Q5) apparently depends on its immediate predecessor. Haviland based his 1629 edition (Q5) on the 1617 (Q3).

Modern Editions

1. Ed. Sir Samuel Egerton Brydges, with Preface, Critical and Biographical. Lee Priory [Kent]: Johnson and Warwick, 1813. xviii, 50 pp. 61 copies. Repr. in *The Bookworm's Garner*, no. VI. Edinburgh: E. & G. Goldsmid, 1889. 86 pp. 100 copies. Based on Q4 (1621).
2. [Ed. J. O. Halliwell-Phillipps]. London: Chiswick Press, 1870. 11 copies. Based on Q2 (1596).
3. *The Shakspere Allusion-Books*. Ed. C. M. Ingleby. The New Shakspere Society. Series 4, no 1. London: 1874. Pt. 1, pp. 1–34. Not in subsequent editions. Based on Q2 (1596).
4. *The Life and Complete Works in Prose and Verse of Robert Greene*, *M.A.*, ed. A. B. Grosart, 15 vols. London: 1881–86. Vol. 12, pp. 95–150. 50 copies. repr. New York: Russell and Russell, 1964. Based on Q2 (1596).
5. *Elizabethan & Jacobean Pamphlets*, ed. George Saintsbury. The

Pocket Library of English Literature, vol 6. London: Percival &
Co., 1892. Pp. 116–63. Based on Q2 (1596).
6. Ed. Reginald Hewitt. Sheldonian Series, no. 4. Oxford: B. H.
Blackwell, 1919. 84 pp. 500 copies. Based on Q4 (1621).
7. Ed. G. B. Harrison. Bodley Head Quartos, no. 6. London: John
Lane; New York: E. P. Dutton, 1923. Repr., New York: Barnes
& Noble, 1966; New York: Burt Franklin, 1970; Westport, Conn.:
Greenwood Press, 1970. Based on Q1 (1592).
8. *A Miscellany of Tracts and Pamphlets*. Ed. A. C. Ward. The World's
Classics, no. 304. London: Humphrey Milford, 1927. Pp. 89–129.
Based on Q1 (1592).
9. Menston, Yorks.: The Scolar Press, 1969. Facs. repr. of the BL
Q1 (1592).
10. Ed. Thomas W. Cobb. Unpubl. doct. diss., Yale Univ., 1977.
Based on Folger Q1 (1592).

The poetry of *Groatsworth* is collected in editions by Alexander Dyce
(1831, 1861), Robert Bell (1856, 1876), J. Churton Collins (1905),
and Tetsumato Hayashi (1977).

This Edition

This edition is based on Q1 (1592) in the Folger Shakespeare Library. Certain features special to printed texts of the sixteenth century
are silently adjusted (ampersands, ligatures, tildes, swash letters,
abbreviations [*qd*, e.g.], the *i, j, u, v* practice, etc.), obvious errors of
composing corrected (wrong-font, wrong-turned type, etc.), and
internal capitals after initials and factotums normalized. Textual notes
record the history of substantive changes in the six early texts and
that of accidentals when the text is poetry or there is some bearing on
meaning. The commentary treats interesting emendations in later editions. The three fonts of the original are reduced to two: the italic of
the preliminary matter and the black letter of the main text are
reproduced in roman, and the alternative fonts of incidental use in the
original are in italic.

Abbreviations

Applegate   Applegate, James Earl. "Classical Allusions in the Prose Works of Robert Greene." Unpubl. Ph.D. diss., The Johns Hopkins Univ., 1954.

Bishops'   *The Holy Byble.* R. Jugge, 1574.

Henry Chettle, *K-HD   Kind-Hartes Dreame* (1592). Ed. G. B. Harrison. 1923. Repr. New York: Barnes & Noble, 1966.

Piers   *Piers Plainness* (1595). *The Descent of Euphues.* Ed. James Winny. Cambridge: University Press, 1957.

Cobb   Cobb, Thomas William, ed. "A Critical Edition of Robert Greene's *Groatsworth of Wit.*" Unpubl. Ph.D. diss., Yale Univ., 1977.

Collins, ed.   *The Plays & Poems of Robert Greene.* Ed. J. Churton Collins. 2 vols. Oxford: Clarendon Press, 1905.

DC-C   "Cuthbert Conny-Catcher." *The Defence of Conny-Catching* (1592). Ed. G. B. Harrison. 1924. Repr. New York: Barnes & Noble, 1966.

Genevan   *The Geneva Bible. A Facsimile of the 1560 Edition.* Introduction by Lloyd E. Berry. Madison: Univ. of Wisconsin Press, 1969.

GGW   *Greene's Groatsworth of Wit* (1592).

Robert Greene, *Disput. A Disputation betweene a Hee Conny-Catcher and a Shee Conny-Catcher* (1592). Ed. G. B. Harrison. 1923. Repr. New York: Barnes & Noble, 1966.

FrF   *Francesco's Fortunes* (1590; that is, *Greene's Never Too Late*, part two).

GMG   *Greene's Mourning Garment* (1590).

GV   *Greene's Vision* (1592; written 1590?).

NDC   *A Notable Discovery of Coosnage* (1591). Ed. G. B. Harrison. 1923. Repr. New York: Barnes & Noble, 1966.

NTL   *Greene's Never Too Late* (1590).

Quip   *A Quip for an Upstart Courtier* (1592). Facs. repr. with an Introduction by Edwin Haviland Miller. Gainesville, FL: Scholars' Facs. & Repr., 1954.

Repent.	Attributed to Robert Greene. *The Repentance of Robert Greene* (1592). Ed. G. B. Harrison. 1923. Repr. New York: Barnes & Noble, 1966.
2C-C	*The Second Part of Conny-Catching* (1591). Ed. G. B. Harrison. 1923. Repr. New York: Barnes & Noble, 1966.
3C-C	*The Thirde & Last Part of Conny-Catching* (1592). Ed. G. B. Harrison. 1923. Repr. New York: Barnes & Noble, 1966.
Works	*The Life and Complete Works in Prose and Verse of Robert Greene, M. A. Cambridge and Oxford.* Ed. A. B. Grosart. 15 vols. London: Huth Library, 1881–86. (Volume and page numbers are given.)

Gabriel Harvey, *FL*   *Foure Letters and Certeine Sonnets, Especially Touching Robert Greene* (1592). Ed. G. B. Harrison. 1922. Repr. New York: Barnes & Noble, 1966.

Works	*The Works of Gabriel Harvey.* Ed. A. B. Grosart. 3 vols. 1884–85. Repr. New York: AMS Press, 1966.
Hoy	Cyrus Hoy. *Introductions, Notes, and Commentaries to Texts in "The Dramatic Works of Thomas Dekker."* 4 vols. Cambridge: University Press, 1980.
N&Q	*Notes and Queries.*
Nashe	*The Works of Thomas Nashe.* Ed. R. B. McKerrow. 5 vols. 1904–10. Repr. with revisions by F. P. Wilson. Oxford: Basil Blackwell, 1958. (Volume and page numbers are given.)
ODEP	*The Oxford Dictionary of English Proverbs.* Rev. by F. P. Wilson. Oxford: Clarendon Press, 1970.
OED	*Oxford English Dictionary* (1989).
RES	*Review of English Studies.*
Stevenson	*The Home Book of Proverbs, Maxims, and Famous Phrases.* Selected and Arranged by Burton Stevenson. New York: Macmillan, 1948.
Tilley	Tilley, Morris Palmer. *A Dictionary of the Proverbs in England in the Sixteenth and Seventeenth Centuries.* Ann Arbor: Univ. of Michigan Press, 1950. Repr. 1966.

Unless otherwise indicated, lineation to Shakespeare's works is to the Riverside Edition; the Bible quoted or referred to, the Bishops' (1574).

GREENE'S GROATSWORTH OF WIT

Bought with a Million of Repentance

(1592)

Attributed to

Henry Chettle and Robert Greene

The Printer to the Gentle Readers.

I have published here Gentle men for your mirth and benefite *Greenes* groates worth of wit. With sundry of his pleasant
discourses, ye have beene before delighted: But nowe hath
death given a period to his pen, onely this happened into my   5
handes which I have published for your pleasures: Accept it
favourably because it was his last birth and not least worth, in
my poore opinion. But I will cease to praise that which is above
my conceipt, and leave it selfe to speak for it selfe: and so abide
your learned censuring.   10

Yours W. W. [1] |A3^r|

---

title] The title echoes a commonplace (Tilley, C689): "He that refuses
to buy counsel cheap shall buy repentance dear." A groat, worth four
pence, and probably the price of *GGW*, was a proverbial pittance (G458:
"Not worth a groat"). There may be a suggestion of the typical price of
medicine: thus "*Groats-worth of health*" (J. Hall, *Virgidemiae*, II.iv, 1598
[ed. 1949], 27); "a groatsworth of physic" (Dekker, *Gull's Hornbook*,
1609 [ed. 1904], 24). Jonson has a character prescribe *GGW* for melancholy (*Epicœne*, IV.iv.118–35 [ed. Herford and Simpson], 5:233).
motto (see frontispiece)] Cf. Tilley, M1010: "Once to have been happy
is misery enough," on which see J. Green, *N&Q* 174 (1938): 436–38.
Cf. *FrF*, 8:128; *Nashe*, 3:116.
[1] W. W.] i.e., William Wright, London bookseller. This epistle uses
three question marks for less urgent and specific marks, no doubt because type was short in font.

To the Gentlemen Readers.

Gentlemen. The Swan sings melodiously before death, that in all his life time useth but a jarring sound. *Greene* though able
15 inough to write, yet deeplyer serched with sicknes than ever heeretofore, sendes you his Swanne like songe, for that he feares he shall never againe carroll to you woonted love layes, never againe discover to you youths pleasures. How ever yet sicknesse, riot, Incontinence, have at once shown their
20 extremitie yet if I recover, you shall all see, more fresh sprigs, then ever sprang from me, directing you how to live, yet not diswading ye from love. This is the last I have writ, and I feare me the last I shall write. And how ever I have beene censured for some of my former bookes,[1] yet Gentlemen I protest, they
25 were as I had speciall information. But passing them, I commend this to your favourable censures, that like an Embrion |A3ᵛ| without shape,[2] I feare me will be thrust into the world. If I live to end it, it shall be otherwise: if not, yet will I commend it to your courtesies, that you may as well be acquainted
30 with my repentant death, as you have lamented my careles course of life. But as *Nemo ante obitum felix,*[3] so *Acta Exitus probat:*[4] Beseeching therefore so to be deemed heereof as I deserve, I leave the worke to your likinges, and leave you to your delightes. |A4ʳ|

---

[1] censured . . . bookes] The cony-catching pamphlets of his last year claim first-hand knowledge of London's underworld. Note *DC-C*: "Was your braine so barraine that you had no other subject?" (11); *K-HD*, 35–36, has Greene defend his choice of topics.

[2] Embrion . . .] i.e., embryo (of a man). Cf. Nashe, *Anatomy*, 1589, 1:4; *Lenten Stuff*, 1599, 3:152–53; *NTL*, 8:6.

[3] Nemo . . . felix] "Call no man happy before his death." Applegate wonders if the phrase, which had proverbial force, reflected Ovid's *Metamorphoses*, 3.136–37.

[4] Acta . . . probat] "The end tests ('proves' or justifies) the deeds (or all)." Applegate cites Ovid's *Heroides*, II.85.

GREENES

GROATES-WORTH

OF WIT.

In an Iland bounded with the Ocean there was somtime a
Cittie situated, made riche by Marchandize, and populous by
long peace, the name is not mentioned in the Antiquarie, or els
worne out by times Antiquitie, what it was it greatly skilles not,
but therein thus it happened.[1] An old new made Gentleman
herein dwelt, of no small credit, exceeding wealth, and large
conscience: hee had gathered from many to bestow upon one,
for though he had two sonnes he esteemed but one, that being
as himselfe, brought up to be golds bondman, was therefore

---

[1] *In an Iland . . . .*] The city name is withheld to make fun of the anti-
quarians' trick of dwelling on names and their origins, especially on
London. This opening echoes Stow's, from *Summary*, 1565 (Ai^r), through
to *Annals* (1–2), signed 26 May 1592, which Stow says (*Summary*, Ai^r)
he "gathered" out of P. Vergil, who uses it starting in 1534. M. C.
Bradbrook thinks Norwich the city meant (*Shakespeare Survey* 15 [1962]:
65), Greene's acknowledged origin. Nothing in the narrative suggests a
city other than London. Nashe attacks "upstart antiquaries" in *Anatomy*,
1589, 1:9, and in *Pierce*, 1592, 1:182–83, which latter, he claims, provoked a response from them (1:154). *In the Antiquarie*, i.e., in antiquity
(*OED*, first of two), or "in the (records of the) antiquarian." Cf. Greene,
Royal Exchange, 1590, 7:222: "wee may boast out of the Antiquaries, that
our Cittie of London . . . is more ancient farre then their Cittie of Venice."

held heire apparant of his il gathered goods.

The other was a Scholler, and maried to a proper Gentlewoman and therfore least regarded, for tis an old sayd saw: To
50 learning and law, thers no greater foe than they that nothing
know[1]: yet |B1ʳ| was not the father altogether unlettered, for
he had good experience in a *Noverint*, and by the universall
tearmes therein contained,[2] had driven many a yoong Gentleman to seeke unknowen countries. Wise he was, for he boare
55 office in his parish[3] and sat as formally in his foxfurd gowne,[4]
as if he had been a very upright dealing Burges: he was religious too, never without a booke at his belt,[5] and a bolt in his
mouthe, readye to shoote through his sinfull neighbor.[6]

And Latin hee had some where learned, which though it
60 were but little, yet was it profitable, for he had this Philosophye
written in a ring, *Tu tibi cura*,[7] which precept he curiously ob-

---

[1] *To learning . . . know*] Cf. Tilley, A331, and McKerrow on its use in
Anatomy, 1589, ed., *Nashe*, 1:35.

[2] *experience . . . contained*] i.e., practice in (the drawing up of) writs
(*OED* cites this first), which began with "*noverint universi.*" The scriv-
ener, which the father either was or made use of, to Stubbes (*Anatomy of
Abuses*, 1583 [facs., 1973], Liᵛ), "is the Instrument wherby the Divell
worketh the frame of this wicked woorke of Usurie."

[3] *office in his parish*] As alderman, presumably.

[4] *foxfurd gowne*] Probably edged, a leading characteristic of the
usurer; see C. T. Wright, *Studies in Philology* 31 (1934): 189–91. In *DC-
C*, 14, "Cuthbert" wonders why Greene does not write against "those
Fox-furd Gentlemen."

[5] *booke . . . belt*] i.e., a Bible attached to his belt. Stubbes gives similar
details of his usurer in *Anatomy*, 1583 (facs., 1973), Hviᵛ.

[6] *bolt . . . neighbor*] Cf. Tilley, F515: "a fool's bolt is soon shot."
Stubbes' usurers "take [God's] word in their mouthes, and yet lyve
cleane contrarie" (*Anatomy*, 1583 [facs., 1973], Hviᵛ).

[7] Tu tibi cura] E. Meyer, comparing Barabas' *Ego mihimet sum semper
proximus*, takes Gorinius' egoism here to be from Gentillet's *Contre-
Machiavel*, 1576 (2d edn., 1579), as "inspired by" Marlowe (*Machiavelli
and the Elizabethan Drama* [1897, repr. 1969], 66–67). M. Praz derives
the charge of avarice from Gentillet (*Flaming Heart* [1958], 92–93). In
Greene's *James IV*, Ateukin is accused of having "annotations upon
Machiavel" (III.ii.53, ed. Sanders); in *Martin's Month's Mind*, G2ʳ
(1589), Martin refers to "my works of Machivell, with my marginall
notes and scholies thereupon"; in *London Prodigal*, D1ᵛ (1910; repr.
1970), Flowerdale, sometimes thought to be Greene, makes similar

served, being in selfelove so religious, as he held it no poynt of charitie to part with any thing, of whiche hee living might make use.

But as all mortall thinges are momentanie, and no certaintie [65] can bee found in this uncertaine world: so *Gorinius*,[1] (for that shall bee this usurers name) after manye a gowtie pang that had pincht his exterior partes,[2] many a curse of the people that mounted into hevens presence, was at last with his last summons, by a deadly disease arrested, wheragainst when hee had [70] long contended, and was by Phisitions given over, he cald his two sonnes before him: and willing to performe the old proverb *Qualis vita finis Ita*,[3] he thus prepard himselfe, and admonished them. My sonnes (for so your mother sayde ye were) and so I assure myselfe one of you is, and of the other I will make [75] no doubt.

You se the time is com, which I thought would |B1ᵛ| never have aprohed and we must now be seperated, I feare never to meete againe. This sixteene yeares dayly have I livde vexed with disease: and might I live sixteene more, howe ever miserably, I [80] should thinke it happye. But death is relentlesse, and will not be intreated:[4] witles, and knowes not what good my gold might doo him: senseles, and hath no pleasure in the delightfull places I would offer him. In briefe, I thinke he hath with this foole my eldest sonne been brought up in the universitie, and therefore [85] accounts that in riches is no vertue.[5] But thou my son, (laying

---

annotations; in *A Knack to Know a Knave*, new in June, 1592, sometimes attr. to Greene, a usurer-father, seeing death and unable to repent, advises his sons to "Carve to yourselves" (line 359, B3ʳ [ed. 1963]).

[1] Gorinius] Lat. for *Greene*.

[2] *gowtie pang* ...] Like his other features, commonplace; see C. T. Wright, *Studies in Philology* 31 (1934): 189–91.

[3] Qualis ... Ita] Cf. Tilley, L263: "Such a life such an end."

[4] *death ... intreated*] Cf. Tilley, D150: "Death when it comes will have no denial." First cit. in *OED* for *relentless*.

[5] *in ... vertue*] Stevenson, p. 1979, quotes Plato: "It's true what is commonly said, rich men can't be good." Scenes such as this, says J. C. Jordan (*Robert Greene* [1915], 63 n.), came to stand for those in which the prodigal tries to gain his father's consent to travel. G. Gascoigne, in *Glass of Government*, made the elder the prodigal, as Cobb notes (ccxxxiii), following a distinction Ascham made: "The eldest beeing yong

then his hand on the yongers head) have thou another spirit:
for without wealth, life is a death: what is gentry if welth be
wanting, but bace servile beggerie. Some comfort yet it is unto
90   me, to thinke how many Gallants sprunge of noble parents,
have croucht to *Gorinius* to have sight of his gold: O gold,
desired gold, admired gold![1] and have lost their patrimonies to
Gorinius, because they have not returned by their day that
adored creature! How manye Schollers have written rymes in
95   *Gorinius* praise, and received (after long capping and reverence)
a sixpeny reward in signe of my superficial liberality. Breefly my
yong *Lucanio*[2] how I have beene revrenst thou seest, when
honester men I confesse have been sett farre off: for to bee rich
is to bee any thing, wise, honest, worshipful, or what not. I tel
100 thee my sonne: when I came first to this Citie my whole
wardrop was onely a sute of white sheepe skins,[3] my wealth an
old groat, my woonning, the wide world. At this instant (o
greefe to part with it) I have in ready |B2^r| coine threescore
thousand pound, in plate and Jewels xv. thousand, in Bondes
105 and specialties as much, in land nine hundred pound by the
yeere: all which, *Lucanio* I bequeath to thee, only I reserve for
Roberto thy wel red brother an old groat, (being the stocke I
first began with) wherewith I wish him to buy a groats-worth of
wit: for he in my life hath reproovd my manner of life, and
110 therefore at my death, shall not be contaminated with corrupt
gaine. Here by the way Gentlemen must I digresse to shewe the
reason of *Gorinius* present speach: *Roberto* being come from the
Academie, to visit his father, there was a great feast provided:
where for table talke, *Roberto* knowing his father and most of

---

men of quicke capacitie do (Parrotte like) very quickly learne the rules
without booke: the yonger beeing somewhat more dull of understanding,
do yet engrave the same within their memories" (ed. Cunliffe [1910], 5).

   [1] *O gold . . . gold!*] Cf. *Piers*, 159: "O gold, adored gold, my soules
cheefe soveraigne," etc., in Ulpian's "dailie execrable Orizons honouring
gold as the cheefest good." *Pierce*, 1592, *Nashe*, 1:159, shares several
details with *GGW* here.

   [2] Lucanio] To suggest *lucre*.

   [3] *sute . . . skins*] With a play on legal *suit*, bonds being made out of
sheep skins. Cf. *1H6*, IV.ii.78–81; *Ham.*, V.i.123. Nashe's Greediness is
"attyred in a Capouch of written parchment" (*Pierce*, 1592, 1:166).

the company to be execrable usurers, invayed mightely against   115
that abhorred vice, insomuche that hee urged teares from divers
of their eyes, and compunction in some of their harts. Dinner
being past, he comes to his father, requesting him to take no
offence at his liberall speach, seeing what he had uttred was
truth. Angry, sonne (said he), no by my honestie (and that is   120
som what I may say to you) but use it still, and if thou canst
perswade any of my neighbours from lending uppon usurie I
shuld have the more customers: to which when *Roberto* would
have replyde hee shut himselfe into his studdy, and fell to tell
over his mony.   125

This was *Robertos* offence: now returne wee to sicke *Gorinius*,
who after he had thus unequally distributed his goods and
possessions, began to aske his sonnes how they liked his be-
questes, either seemed agreed, and *Roberto* urged him with
|B2ᵛ| nothing more than repentance of his sinn: loke to thine   130
owne said he, fonde boy, and come my *Lucanio*, let me give
thee good counsell before my death: as for you sir, your bookes
are your counsellors, and therefore to them I bequeathe you.
Ah *Lucanio*, my onely comfort, because I hope thou wilt as thy
father be a gatherer, let me blesse thee before I dye. Multiply in 135
welth my sonne by any meanes thou maist, onely flye Al-
chymie, for therein are more deceites than her beggerlye Ar-
tistes have words, and yet are the wretches more talkative than
women. But my meaning is, thou shouldest not stand on conscience in causes of profit, but heap treasure upon treasure,[1] for 140
the time of neede: yet seem to be devout, els shalt thou be held
vyle, frequent holy exercises[2] grave companie, and above al use
the conversation of yoong Gentlemen, who are so wedded to
prodigalitie, that once in a quarter necissitie knocks at their
chamber doores: profer them kindnesse to relieve their wants,   145
but be sure of good assurance: give faire wordes till dayes of
paiment come, and then use my course, spare none: what

---

[1] *heap ... treasure*] Echoing (ironically) biblical warnings: Ps. 39:6,
Matt. 6:19–20, Jas. 5:3.

[2] *holy exercises*] "The exercises of praying, singing of psalms, inter-
preting, and prophesying" (*OED*, 1574). The comma after *exercises* in
other Qq seems attractive, but the genitive makes sense.

though they tell of conscience (as a number will talke) looke but into the dealinges of the world, and thou shalt see it is but idle words. Seest thou not many perish in the streetes, and fall to theft for neede: whom small succor woulde releeve, then where is conscience, and why art thou bound to use it more than other men? Seest thou not daylie forgeries, perjuries, oppressions, rackinges[1] of the poore, raisinges of rents, inhauncing of duties even by them that should be al conscience, if they ment as they speake: |B3ʳ| but *Lucanio* if thou read well this booke (and with that hee reacht him *Machiavels* workes at large[2]) thou shalt se, what tis to be so foole-holy as to make scruple of conscience where profit presents it selfe.

Besides, thou hast an instance by thy threed bare brother here, who willing to do no wrong, hath lost his childes right: for who woulde wish any thinge to him, that knowes not how to use it.

So much *Lucanio* for conscience: and yet I know not whats the reason, but some-what stinges mee inwardly when I speake of it. I father, said *Roberto*, it is the worme of conscience,[3] that urges you at the last houre to remember your life, that eternall life may followe your repentance. Out foole (sayd this miserable father) I feele it not now,[4] it was onelye a stitch. I will forwarde with my exhortation to *Lucanio*. As I said my sonne, make spoyle of yoong Gallants, by insinuating thy selfe amongst them, and be not mooved to thinke their Auncestors were famous, but consider thine were obscure, and that thy father was the first Gentleman of the Name: *Lucanio*, thou art yet a

---

[1] *rackinges*] oppressions by extortions or exactions (*OED*). Cf. Stubbes, *Anatomy* (facs., 1973), Iviiijʳ: "So (likewise) Landlords make marchandise of their pore tenants, racking their rents, raising their fines."

[2] *Machiavels . . . large*] i.e., in full, unabridged. That is, not Gentillet's *Contre-Machiavel*, the popular version. Five different works of Machiavelli in Italian were printed by Wolfe with false imprints between 1584 and 1588. See note to "*Tu tibi cura*" (line 61), and Appendix E.

[3] *worme of conscience*] The usurer in Lodge's *Catharos*, 1591 (ed. 1883), II.ii.33, "shall have in recompense of his villanie, a worme which shal feede upon him, and tyre upon his conscience."

[4] *feele it not now*] So Grosart (ed., 12:298) for "feele it now" of the Qq.

Bacheler, and soe keepe thee till thou meete with one that is
thy equal, I meane in wealth: regarde not beautie, it is but a
bayte to entice thy neighbors eye:[1] and the most faire are com-
monlye most fond, use not too many familiars, for few proove
frendes, and as easie it is to weigh the wind,[2] as to dive into the
thoughtes of worldlye glosers.[3] I tell thee *Lucanio*, I have seene
four-scoore winters besides the od seven, yet saw I never him,
that I esteemed as my friend but gold, that desired creature,
whom I have so deerly loved, |B3ᵛ| and found so firme a frind,
as nothing to me having it hath beene wanting. No man but
may thinke deerly of a true frend,[4] and so do I of it, laying it
under sure locks, and lodging my heart there-with.

But now (Ah my *Lucanio*) now must I leave it, and to thee
I leave it with this lessen, love none but thy selfe, if thou wilt
live esteemd. So turning him to his studdy, where his cheife
treasure lay, he loud cryde out in the wise mans woords, *O
mors quam amara*, O death how bitter is thy memory to him
that hath al pleasures in this life,[5] and so with two or three
lamentable grones hee left his life: and to make short worke,
was by *Lucanio* his sonne interd, as the custome is with some
solemnitie: But leaving him that hath left the world to him that
censureth of every worldly man,[6] passe wee to his sonnes: and se
how his long laid up store is by *Lucanio* lookyd into. The youth
was of condition simple, shamfast, and flexible to any counsaile, which *Roberto* perceiving, and pondering howe little was
lefte to him, grew into an inward contempt of his fathers unequall legacie, and determinate resolution to work *Lucanio* al
possible injurie, hereupon thus converting the sweetness of his
studdye to the sharpe thirst of revenge, he (as Envie is seldome

---

[1] *thy neighbors eye*] An echo of Ex. 20:17, Lev. 18:20, 20:10.

[2] *as easie . . . wind*] Cf. Tilley, W417: "He that weighs the wind must
have steady hand."

[3] *dive . . . glosers*] Cf. *R3*, III.i.8: "div'd into the world's deceit."

[4] *my friend . . . frend*] Inverting "A true friend a great treasure"
(Tilley, F719).

[5] *wise . . . life*] From the "Wisdom" of Ecclesiasticus 41:1-2 (Vulgate): "*O mors quam amara est memoria tua homini pacem habenti in
substantiis suis. . . .*"

[6] *him that censureth . . . man*] that passes judgment on (that is, God).

idle[1]) sought out fit companions to effect his unbrotherly reso-
205 lution. Neither in such a case is ill company far to seek, for the
Sea hath scarce so many jeoperdies, as populous Citties have
deceiving Syrens, whose eies are Adamants,[2] whose words are
witchcraftes, whose doores lead downe to death.[3] With one of
these female serpents[4] *Roberto* consorts, and |B4ʳ| they con-
210 clude what ever they compassed equally to sharre to their
contentes. This match made, *Lucanio* was by his brother
brought to the bush, where he had scarse pruned his winges,[5]
but hee was fast limd,[6] and *Roberto* had what he expected. But
that wee may keepe forme, you shall heare howe it fortuned.
215   *Lucanio* being on a time verie pensive, his brother brake with
him in these termes. I wonder *Lucanio* why you are disconso-
late, that want not any thinge in the worlde that may worke
your content. If wealth may delight a man, you are with that
sufficently furnisht: if credit may procure any comfort, your
220 word I knowe well, is as well accepted as any mans obligation:
in this Citie, are faire buildings and pleasant gardens, and cause
of solace, of them I am assured you have your choyce. Consider brother you are yoong, then plod not altogether in medi-
tating on our fathers precepts: which howsever they savored of
225 profit, were most unsaverly to one of your yeares applied. You
must not thinke but sundrye marchants of this Citie expect
your company, sundry Gentlemen desire your familiaritie, and
by conversing with such, you wil be accounted a Gentleman:

---

[1] *Envie . . . idle*] Cf. Stevenson, 701: "Envy hath no holidays." *Envy*
was close in sense to our "malice" or "hatred."

[2] *Adamants*] magnets (as often in Greene), with a possibility of the
added sense diamonds, natural opposite of magnets, exploiting a confusion between meanings (see *OED*).

[3] *doores . . . death*] From Prov. 7:27. The image occurs at lines 316
and 847, and in *Disput.*, 5.

[4] *female serpents*] Common for malice hidden under a pleasant dispo-
sition. Cf. J. Ferne, *Blazon of Gentry*, 1586, pt. 2, 40: "a Viper [is used]
to signifie a common woman or harlot lying in the way, to sting men
with the contagion of her wantonnes and lust"; *Disput.*, 71.

[5] *pruned his winges*] trimmed (or dressed) his feathers (with his beak),
fig. for made himself attractive.

[6] *brought . . . limd*] Small birds were caught by smearing twigs with
lime. Cf. *GMG*, 9:163, 178; *Disput.*, 10; Prov. 7:22–23.

otherwise a pesant, if ye live thus obscurely. Besides, which I
had almost forgot and then had al the rest beene nothing, you   230
are a man by nature furnished with all exquisite proportion,
worthy the love of any courtly lady, be she never so amorous:
you have wealth to maintaine her, of women not little longed
for: wordes to court her you shall not want, for my selfe will be
|B4^v| your secretarie.[1] Breefely why stand I to distinguish   235
abilitie in perticularities,[2] when in one word it may be said
which no man can gainsay, *Lucanio* lacketh nothing to delight
a wife, nor any thing but a wife to delight him? My yoong
maister being thus clawd, and pufft up[3] with his owne praise,
made no longer delay, but having on his holidaie hose hee   240
trickt himselfe up and like a fellowe that meant good sooth,[4] he
clapt hys brother on the shoulder and said, Faith brother *Roberto*, and ye say the worde lets goe seeke a wife while tis hoat,
both of us together, Ile pay well, and I dare tourne you loose to
say as well as any of them all: well, Ile doo my best, said *Rober-*   245
to, and since ye are so forwarde lets goe nowe and try your
good fortune.

    With this foorth they walke, and *Roberto* went directly to-
ward the house where *Lamilia*[5] (for so wee call the Curtizan)
kept her hospitall, which was in the suburbes of the Citie,[6]   250

---

[1] *secretarie*] "One who writes (on a particular occasion) for another"
(*OED*, citing this only).

[2] *distinguish . . . perticularities*] divide (the evidence of your) fitness (for
such an undertaking) into specifics.

[3] *clawd . . . up*] flattered and made proud.

[4] *fellowe . . . sooth*] partner true to his word.

[5] Lamilia] Dim. of *Lamia*, beautiful witch who devoured the men she
lured, and a common name for a prostitute, probably from Demetrius
Poliorcetes' famous courtesan. *Lamia* is the prostitute in G. Whetstone's
Promos and Cassandra, 1578, in whose *Rock of Regard*, 1576, Paulus
Plasmos complains of a faithless lady named *Laymos*. On names in *Rock* see
M. Eccles, *RES* 33 (1982): 386. Cobb thinks (ccxvi–vii, ccc–ii) that *GGW*
may rely on *Rock*, especially on the section "Orchard of Repentance."

[6] *hospitall . . . Citie*] i.e., "house of entertainment" (*OED* 5), euph.
for brothel. Probably in the north of London, either Shoreditch or the
vicinity of Bishopsgate, near "the *Spittle*" (see *Pierce*, 1592, *Nashe*, 1:217;
McKerrow's note, 3:81). "In place of this hospital ['the late dissolved
priory and hospital commonly called St. Mary Spittle'] and near adjoin-
ing, are now many fair houses built for receipt and lodging of worshipful

pleasantly seated, and made more delectable by a pleasaunt garden[1] wherin it was scituate. No soner come they within ken, but Mistris *Lamilia* like a cunning angler made readye her change of baytes that shee might effect *Lucanios* bane: and to begin she discovered from her window her beauteous enticing face, and taking a lute in her hand that shee might the rather allure, shee soung this sonnet with a delicious voyce, |C1ʳ|

255

Lamilias song.

> Fie fie on blind fancie,
> It hinders youths joy:
> Faire virgins learne by me,
> To count love a toy.[2]
> When love learnd first the A B C of delight,[3]
> And knew no figures, nor conceited phrase:
> He simply gave to due desert her right,
> He led not lovers in darke winding wayes,
>   He plainely wild to love, or flatly answerd no,
>   But now who lists to prove shall find it nothing so,
>   Fie fie then on fancie,
>   It hinders youths joy,
>   Faire virgins learne by me,
>   To count love a toy.

260

265

270

> For since he learnd to use the Poets pen,
> He learnd likewise with smoothing words to faine,
> Witching chast eares[4] with trothles tungs of men,
> And wronged faith with falshood and disdaine.

275

---

persons" (Stow, *Survey of London*, 1603 [ed. 1912], 150–51).

  [1] *garden*] Perhaps a glance at the "garden houses," a by-word for illicit sex and located in the fields and suburbs.

  [2] Fie ... toy.] Cf. *FrF*, 8:213: "Fie on Love, it is a toy."

  [3] A B C ...] Alluding to the primer (pronounced *Absey*).

  [4] Witching chast eares] E. Guilpin has lascivious poets "Filthing chast eares with theyr pens *Gonorrhey*" (*Skialetheia*, 1598, *Sat. Pre.*, 60 [ed. Carroll]).

He gives a promise now, anon he sweareth no,
Who listeth for to prove shall find his changings so,
Fie fie then on fancie,
It hinders youthes joy, 280
Faire virgins learne by me,
To count love a toy. |C1ᵛ|

While this painted sepulcher[1] was shadowing her corrupting
guile, Hiena-like alluring to destruction,[2] *Roberto* and *Lucanio*
under her windowe kept even pace with every stop of her 285
instrument, but especially my yoong Ruffler, (that before time
like a birde in a cage had beene prentise for three lives or one
and twentie yeares at lest to extreame Avarice his deceased
father). O twas a world to see howe hee sometyme simperd it,
striving to sett a countenance on his new turnd face,[3] that it 290
might seeme of wainscot proofe,[4] to behold her face without
blushing: anone he would stroke his bow-bent-leg,[5] as if he
ment to shoote love arrows from his shins: then wypt his chin
(for his beard was not yet growen) with a gold wrought hand-
kercher, whence of purpose he let fall a handfull of Angels. 295
This golden shower[6] was no sooner raind, but *Lamilia* ceast her
song, and *Roberto* (assureing himselfe the foole was caught[7])
came to *Lucanio* (that stood now as one that had stard *Medusa*

---

[1] *painted sepulcher*] From Matt. 23:27. Used often by Greene. Material here reappears in *Ratsey's Ghost* (1605), A2ᵛ (facs., 1932).

[2] *Hiena-like . . . destruction*] By laughing or by imitation, the hyena enticed its victims to death. Cf. S. Gosson, *School of Abuse*, 1579, A2ʳ (facs., 1973); *FrF*, 8:138; *GMG*, 9:191, 200; *Planetomachia*, 5:53; *Perimedes*, 7:63.

[3] *new turnd face*] i.e., turned aside, out of embarrassment, probably with metaphoric "turned" (as on a lathe). *To set a face* was often followed by a comparison with some hard substance, as at Isaiah 50:7. Cf. *DC-C*, 7.

[4] *of wainscot proofe*] i.e., resistant to change, like oak paneling.

[5] *bow-bent-leg*] i.e., "bowleg." From the itch of pleasure; cf. "scratch his scabd elbowes at this speach" in *Nashe*, 2:219, with Wilson's note, 5:36.

[6] *golden shower*] Alluding to Jove's wooing of Danae.

[7] *foole was caught*] Cf. similar phrasing in *GMG*, 9:176 (in the brothel).

300 in the face[1]) and awaked him from his amazement with these
wordes. What, in a traunce brother? whence springs these
dumps? are ye amazd at this object?[2] or long ye to become loves
subject? Is there not difference betweene this delectable life,
and the imprisonment you have all your life hethertoo indured?
305 If the sight and hearing of this harmonyous beautie worke in
you effects of wonder, what will the possession of so devine an
essence, wherein beautie and Art dwell in their perfectest
excellence. Brother, said *Lucanio*, lets use fewe wordes, and
shee be no more then a woman, I trust youle helpe |C2ʳ| me
to win her: and if you doe, well, I say no more but I am yours
310 till death us depart,[3] and what is mine shall be yours world
without end Amen.[4]

Roberto smiling at his simplenes helpte him to gather uppe
his dropt gold, and without anye more circumstance, led him to
Lamilias house: for of such places it may be said as of hell:

315 *Noctes atque dies patet atri ianua ditis.*[5]

So their dores are ever open to entice youth to distruction.[6]
They were no sooner entred but *Lamilia* her selfe like a sec-
onde *Helen*, court like begins to salute *Roberto*, yet did her
wandring eie glance often at *Lucanio*: the effect of her intertain-
320 ment consisted in these tearmes, that to her simple house
Signor *Roberto* was welcome, and his brother the better welcom

---

[1] *stard ... face*] Cf. *Mamillia*, 2:22; *Perimedes*, 7:78; *NTL*, 8:57, 84.
On this variation from head as evidence of hoax, see Warren B. Austin,
in L. Marder, *Shakespeare Newsletter* 16 (Sept. 1966): 29–30, and Cobb's
response, cccxvii–iii.

[2] *object*] sight, especially one exciting love, spectacle (*OED* 3.b, citing
Perimedes, 1588, 7:79). *OED* apparently recognizes *subject-object* once
before 17c., and that in Lat. (1513).

[3] *till ... depart*] From the marriage pledge in early editions of *Book of
Common Prayer*.

[4] *world ... Amen*] Last phrase of Gloria Patri in the services of the
English Church.

[5] Noctes ... ditis.] "The door of black Pluto is open night and day"
(*Aeneid*, VI.127). Repeated in *Ratsey's Ghost* (1605), A2ᵛ (facs., 1932),
with other details from this section.

[6] *dores ... distruction*] This image also occurs at lines 208 (see note)
and 847.

for his sake: albeit his good report confirmde by his present demeaner were of it selfe enough to give him deserved entertainement in any place how honorable soever: mutuall thankes returnd, they led this prodigall child[1] into a parlor garnished with goodly portratures of amiable personages: nere which an excellent consort of musike began at their entraunce to play. *Lamilia* seeing *Lucanio* shamefast, tooke him by the hand, and tenderly wringing him used these wordes. Beleeve me Gentleman, I am very sorie that our rude entertainment is such, as no way may worke your content, for this I have noted since your first entering that your countenance hath beene heavie, and the face being the glasse of the hart, assures me the same is not quiet: would ye wish any thing heere that might content you, say |C2ᵛ| but the word, and assure ye of present diligence to effect your full delight. *Lucanio* being so farre in love, as he perswaded himselfe without her grant he could not live,[2] had a good meaninge to utter his minde but wanting fit wordes, he stood like a trewant that lackt a prompter, or a plaier that being out of his part at his first entrance, is faine to have the booke to speak what he should performe. Which *Roberto* perceiving, replied thus in his behalfe: Madame the Sunnes brightnesse daisleth the beholders eies, the majestie of Gods, amazeth humane men, *Tullie* Prince of Orators once fainted though his cause were good,[3] and hee that tamed monsters stoode amated at Beauties ornaments[4]: Then blame not this yoong man though

325

330

335

340

345

---

[1] *prodigall child*] The prodigal came to stand for someone seduced and fleeced in a brothel. Cf. *Disput.*, 5, 28, 36, 72.

[2] *without ... live*] Cf. similar phrasing in *GMG*, 9:176.

[3] Tullie ... *good*] Perhaps in defense of Milo (Plutarch, *Lives of the Noble Grecians and Romans*, xxxv), or else confused with Demosthenes against Harpalus (Plutarch, xxv). Applegate (*s.v.* Cicero) suspects a fabrication. Cf. *OED* (Amated, 1656): "[Demosthenes was] sometimes so amated that he had not a word to say." Cicero in love cannot speak in *NTL*, 8:85.

[4] *hee ... ornaments*] Probably Hercules with Omphale or Iole, not Perseus, a common example of what love can do to the manly. On the confusion over the females see V. Skretkowicz, *N&Q*, n.s. 27 (1980): 306–10. Applegate, missing this one, notes five references in Greene. F. G. Hubbard traces the image in Greene, in *Shakespeare Studies* (1916), 17–35. But cf. *Ciceronis Amor*, 7:210: "At this reply *Fabius* stoode so

he replied not, for he is blinded with the beautie of your sunne
darkening eies, made mute with the celestiall organe of your
voyce, and feare of that rich ambush of amber colored dartes,
350 whose poyntes are leveld against his hart.[1] Well Signor *Roberto*,
said shee, how ever you interpret their sharpe levell, be sure
they are not bent to doo him hurt, and but that modestie
blindes us poore maydens from uttering the inward sorrow of
our mindes, perchance the cause of greefe is ours how ever
355 men do colour, for as I am a virgin I protest, (and therewithall
shee tainted her cheekes with a vermilion blush[2]) I never saw
Gentleman in my life in my eie so gratious as is *Lucanio*; only
this is my greefe, that either I am dispised for that he scornes to
speak, or els (which is my greater sorrow) I feare he cannot
360 speake. Not speake, Gentlewoman, quoth *Lu-*|C3r|*canio*? that
were a jest indeed, yes I thanke God I am sound of wind and
lym, only my hart is not as it was wont: but and you be as good
as your word that will soone be well, and so craving ye of more
acquaintance, in token of my plaine meaning receive this dia-
365 mond, which my old father lovd deerely: and with that delivered her a ringe wherein was a poynted diamonde of wonderfull
worth. Which she accepting with a lowe conge, returnd him a
silke Riband for a favour tyde with a true loves knot,[3] which he
fastened under a faire Jewel on his Bever felt.[4]
370 After this *Diomedis et Glauci permutatio*,[5] my yong master

---

amated as if hee had beene an unwelcome guest at the feast of *Perseus*";
and, above, lines 297–98: "one that had stard *Medusa* in the face."

[1] *ambush . . . hart*] From her blond hair. Amber was thought to
attract lovers (*OED* 4).

[2] *tainted . . . blush*] Cf. similar phrasing in *NTL*, 8:71, 93; *GMG*,
9:155.

[3] *true loves knot*] Complex, ornamental form (either a double-looped
bow or a knot formed of two loops interwined) used as a symbol of love
(*OED*). Discussed by L. Hotson in *Mr W. H.* (1964), 168–70, 180–81,
and elsewhere.

[4] *Bever felt*] Hoy (2:237) shows that this hat was expensive and an
especial mark of the gallant, quoting *DC-C*, 59.

[5] *Diomedis . . . permutatio*] "exchange of Diomedes and Glaucus,"
i.e., at a loss based on cowardliness, "renowned proverbially" (Stephanus,
in Applegate), based on *Iliad*, VI.234–36. Greene alludes to the story in
Gwydonius, 4:132.

waxed crancke, and the musike continuing, was very forward in
dauncing, to shew his cunning: and so desiring them to play on
a hornepipe, laid on the pavement lustely with his leaden
heeles, corvetting, like a steede of *Signor Roccoes* teaching,[1] and
wanted nothing but bels, to be a hobbyhorse in a morrice.[2] Yet   375
was he soothed in his folly, and what ever he did *Lamilia* counted excellent: her prayse made him proude, in so much that if
hee had not beene intreated, hee would rather have died in his
daunce, then left off to shew his mistris delight. At last reason-
ably perswaded, seeing the table furnished, hee was content to   380
cease, and settle him to his victuals, on which (having before
labored) hee fed lustely, especially of a Woodcocke pye,[3]
wherewith *Lamilia* his carver, plentifully plied him. Full dishes
having furnisht empty stomackes, and *Lucanio* therby got leisure to talke, falles to discourse of his wealth, his landes, his   385
bondes, his ability, |C3ᵛ| and how himselfe with all he had,

---

[1] *his leaden ... teaching*] To *curvet* was to leap with both fore-legs
first, equally advanced, and then with both hind-legs before the fore-legs
returned to the ground. Dancing was one feat of a bay-gelding *Morocco*
trained and exhibited by one Banks, perhaps from as early as 1588; see
McKerrow, on *Nashe*, 2:230. S. H. Atkins, *N&Q* 167 (1934): 39–44,
does not include *GGW* among almost sixty references. The first clear
reference to Banks' horse (*Nashe*, 2:230, by 27 June 1593) implies that
performances had stopped, which W. Milgate (ed., Donne's *Satires*
[1967], 124) takes to mean because of the plague. *OED* gives 1664 first
for *sb.* "in the names of things coming (or supposed to have originally
come) from Morocco." F. P. Wilson thought McKerrow incorrect in his
guess that this refers, through some play like *Ma(ster) Rocco*, to Banks'
horse. Wilson noted (from 1599, *Nashe*, 5:36) that a well-known teacher of
fencing named Rocco, in London for thirty years, taught his pupils to
"weare leaden soales in their shoes, the better to bring them to nimblenesse
of feet in their fight." It may refer to both teachers at once.
[2] *wanted ... morrice*] The figure "represented by a man equipped
with as much pasteboard as was sufficient to form the head and hinder
parts of a horse, the quadrupedal defects being concealed by a long
mantle or footcloth, like the housing on a horse, that nearly touched the
ground. The performer ... exerted all his skill in burlesque horse-
manship" (Douce, in Hoy, 3:246–47). Dropped from the May games
because of its lewd movements. See V. Alford, *Hobby Horse and Other
Animal Masks* (1978).
[3] *Woodcocke pye*] The woodcock was the type of credulous fool-
ishness.

was at madame *Lamilias* disposing: desiring her afore his brother to tell him simply what she meant. *Lamilia* replied, My sweet *Lucanio,* how I esteeme of thee mine eies do witnes, that like
390 handmaides, have attended thy beauteous face, ever since I firste behelde thee: yet seeing love that lasteth, gathereth by degrees his liking: let this for that suffice, if I finde thee firme, *Lamilia* wilbe faithfull: if fleeting, shee must of necessity be infortunate: that having never seene any whome before she
395 could affect, she should be of him[1] injuriously forsaken. Nay, said *Lucanio,* I dare say my brother here will give his woord: for that I accept your own, said *Lamilia*: for with me your credite is better than your brothers. *Roberto* brake off their amorous prattle with this speech. Sith either of you are of other so fond
400 at the first sight, I doubt not but time will make your love more firme. Yet madame *Lamilia* although my brother and you bee thus forward, some crosse chaunce may come: for *Multa cadunt inter calicem supremaque labra.*[2] And for a warning to teach you both wit, Ile tell you an old wives tale.[3]
405 Before ye goe on with your tale (quod mistris *Lamilia*) let me give ye a caveat by the wey, which shall be figured in a fable.

Lamilias Fable.[4]

The Foxe on a time[5] came to visite the Gray, partly for kin-

---

[1] *of him*] by him.

[2] Multa ... labra] Usually *labra*; *labe* of the first Qq may stand for *labem*. The English occurs in Greene at 2:234, 4:291, 5:88, 125, 173, 7:81, and *Disput.*, 18–19.

[3] *old wives tale*] i.e., trifling, fanciful. It probably implied a serious message; cf. Horace's *anilis fabellas* (*Satires,* II.vi.77–78). That "*Robertoes Tale*" is of an old wife justifies the phrase here.

[4] Lamilias Fable.] For the covert meaning, see Appendix C. An Aesopic form combines with a Reynard-like story based on the traditional deceit of the fox toward the badger, explaining the hostility between badgers and dogs. Apparently Lamilia (the Ewe) is anxious lest she be sacrificed to Roberto's (the Fox's) greed—and be cut out of the take. Cobb (clxxxi–iv) discusses the relevance of the fable to the narrative.

[5] *Foxe on a time*] Formulaic (cf. *Nashe,* 1:221), as is the assertion of kinship on the part of the fox.

dered cheefly for craft: and finding the hole emptie of all other company, saving only one Badger enquired the cause of his solitarinesse: hee dis- | C4^r | cribed, the sodaine death of his dam and sire with the rest of his consortes. The Fox made a Friday face,[1] counterfeiting sorrow: but concludinge that deaths stroke was unevitable perswaded him to seeke som fit mate wherwith to match. The badger soone agreed, so forth they went, and in their way met with a wanton[2] ewe stragling[3] from the fold: the foxe bad the Badger play the tall stripling, and strout on his tiptoes: for (quod he) this ewe is lady of al these lawnds and her brother cheefe belweather of sundry flockes. To bee short, by the Foxes perswasion there would bee a perpetuall league, betweene her harmeles kindred, and all other devouring beastes, for that the Badger was to them all allied: seduced she yeelded, and the Fox conducted thém to the Badgers habitation. Wher drawing her aside under color of exhortation, puld out her throat to satisfie his greedy thirst. Here I shoulde note, a yoonge whelpe[4] that viewed their walke, infourmed the shepheardes of what hapned. They followed, and trained the Foxe and Badger to the hole, the Foxe afore had craftely convaid himselfe away, the shepheards found the Badger raving for the ewes murther, his lamentation being held for counterfet, was by the shepherds dogs werried. The Foxe escaped: the Ewe was spoiled, and ever since betweene the Badgers and dogs hath continued a mortall enmitie: And now be advized, *Roberto* (quod she) go forward with your tale, seek not by sly insinuation to turne our mirth to sorrow. Go to *Lamilia* (quod he) you feare what I meane not, but howe ever yee take it, Ile forward with my tale. | C4^v |

---

[1] *Friday face*] i.e., grave or gloomy expression (*OED*, citing this first).

[2] *wanton*] (1) amorous, (2) refractory. Cf. *Disput.*, 44; Hosea 4:16 (Coverdale).

[3] *stragling*] "as an adj. expressing contempt; often used, and quite characteristic of Greene" (T. H. Dickinson, ed., *Robert Greene* [1909], lvi).

[4] *yoonge whelpe*] Since *whelp* meant "young dog," *yoonge* may suggest the name Young.

Robertoes Tale.[1]

In the North partes there dwelt an olde Squier, that had a
young daughter his heire; who had (as I knowe Madam *Lamilia*
you have had) many youthfull Gentlemen that long time sued
to obtaine her love. But she knowing her own perfections (as
women are by nature proud) would not to any of them vouchsafe favour: insomuch that they perceiving her relentlesse,
shewed themselves not altogether witlesse, but left her to her
fortune, when they found her frowardnes. At last it fortuned
among other strangers, a Farmers sonne visited her Fathers
house: on whom at the first sight she was enamoured, he likewise on her. Tokens of love past betweene them, either acquainted others parentes of their choise, and they kindly gave
their consent. Short tale to make, married they were, and great
solempnitie was at the wedding feast. A yong Gentleman, that
had beene long a suiter to her, vexing that the Sonne of a
Farmer should bee so preferd, cast in his minde by what
meanes (to marre their merriment) hee might steale away the
Bride. Hereupon he confers with an olde Beldam, called Mother *Gunby*, dwelling thereby, whose counsell having taken, he
fell to his practise, and proceeded thus. In the after noone,
when dauncers were verie busie, he takes the Bride by the
hande, and after a turne or two, tels her in her eare, he had a
secret to impart unto her, appointing her in any wise in the evening to find a time to confer with him: she promist she would,
and so they parted. Then goes hee to the Bridegroome, and
with |D1[r]| protestations of entire affect, protests that the great
sorrowe hee takes at that which hee must utter, wheron depended his especiall credit, if it were known the matter by him
should be discovered. After the Bridegrooms promise of se-
crecie, the gentleman tels him, that a frend of his received that

---

[1] Robertoes Tale.] I find no source for this story of the slandered
bridegroom. Bed substitution appears often. S. L. Wolff, in *Greek Romances
in Elizabethan Prose Fiction* (1912; repr. 1961), 406–7, thinks the circumstance suggested by Achilles Tatius' *Clitophon and Leucippe*, II.xx–xxii. B.
Richardson, in *Yearbook of English Studies* 10 (1980): 164, finds a Gunby
family in Snaith, Yorks., where she detects other Greene connections.

morning from the Bride a Letter, wherein shee willed him[1] with
some sixteene horse to await her comming at a Parke side, for
that she detested him in her heart as a base countrey hynde,
with whome her Father compeld her to marry. The Bridegroome almost out of his wits, began to bite his lip. Nay, sayth
the Gentleman, if you will by me bee advizde, you shall salve
her credit, win her by kindnes, and yet prevent her wanton
complot. As how, said the Bridegroome?[2] Mary thus, saide the
Gentleman: In the evening (for till the guests be gone, she
intends not to gad[3]) get you on horsebacke, and seeme to bee of
the companie that attendes her comming. I am appoynted to
bring her from the house to the Parke, and from thence fetch a
winding compasse[4] of a mile about, but to turne unto olde
Mother *Gunbyes* house, where her Lover my friend abydes:
when she alights, I will conduct her to a chamber farre from his
lodging; but when the lights are out, and shee expects her
adulterous copesmate, your selfe (as reason is) shall prove her
bedfellow, where privately you may reproove her, and in the
morning earely returne home without trouble. As for the Gentleman my friend, I will excuse her absence to him, by saying,
she mockt me with her Mayde in steade of her selfe, whome
when I knew at her alighting, I disdained to bring her unto his
presence. The Bridegroome gave his hande it shoulde be so.
|D1ᵛ|

Now by the way you must understand, this Mother *Gunby*
had a daughter, who all that day sate heavily at home with a
willow garland,[5] for that the Bridegroome (if hee had dealt

470

475

480

485

490

495

---

¹ *willed him*] desired, requested him (i.e., the gentleman's "friend,"
the fictitious lover).

² *Bridegroome?*] "In black letter books printed in England about
1580–90, . . . we sometimes find a curious query-mark [as here in Q1]
resembling an acute accent followed by a colon" (McKerrow, *Introduction to Bibliography* [1928], 316).

³ *gad*] go, with the added fig. sense "from the true path," "stray"
(*OED* 2). Cf. *Disput.*, 49; Tilley, W695: "Women and hens are lost by
gadding."

⁴ *fetch . . . compasse*] take a circuitous course. Cf. *NTL*, 8:37.

⁵ *willow garland*] Emblem of disappointed lovers; cf. *FrF*; 8:220;
GMG, 9:156.

faithfully) should have wedded her before any other. But men (*Lamilia*) are unconstant, money now a dayes makes the match, or else the match is marde.

But to the matter: the Bridegroome and the Gentleman thus
500 agreed: he tooke his time, conferd with the Bride, perswaded her that her husband (notwithstanding his faire shew at the marriage) had sworne to his olde sweet heart, their neighbour *Gunbyes* daughter, to bee that night her bedfellow: and if she would bring her Father, his Father, and other friendes to the
505 house at midnight, they should find it so.

At this the young Gentlewoman, inwardly vext to bee by a peasant so abusde, promist if she saw likelyhood of his slipping away, that then she would doo according as he directed.

All this thus sorting, the old womans daughter was trickly
510 attyrde ready to furnish this pageant, for her old mother provided all things necessary.

Well, Supper past, dauncing ended, and the guests would home, and the Bridegroome pretending to bring some friend of his home, got his horse, and to the Parke side he rode, and
515 staide with the horsemen that attended the Gentleman.

Anon came *Marian* like mistris Bride,[1] and mounted behind the Gentleman, away they post, fetch their compasse, and at last alight at the olde wives house, where sodenly she is convayd to her chamber, and the bridegroome sent to keep her
520 company, wher he had scarse devisd how |D2ʳ| to begin his exhortation: but the Father of his Bryde knockt at the chamber doore. At which being somewhat amazed, yet thinking to turne it to a jeast, sith his Wife (as hee thought) was in bed with him, hee opened the doore, saying: Father, you are hartily welcome,
525 I wonder how you found us out heere; this devise to remoove

----

[1] Marian ... *Bride*] i.e., Gunby's daughter dressed like the bride. *Marian* was type-name for a simple country girl, as in *Cobbler of Canterbury* (1590). Maid Marian, companion of Robin Hood in the May Day pageants and Morris dances, was danced lasciviously by a boy dressed up. Cf. H. Crosse, *Virtue's Commonwealth*, 1603 (ed. 1878), 77: "every Countrey-wench that hath but foure nobles a yeare and shiftes, must be trimly trickt up like mayde Marryan in a Morrice daunce, ... though she get it with shiftes; but the shifts that makes her laugh, sendes her home by weeping crosse."

our selves, was with my wives consent, that wee might rest quiet-
ly without the Maides and Batchelers disturbing. But wheres
your Wife, said the Gentleman? why heere in bed, saide hee. I
thought (quoth the other) my daughter had beene your wife,
for sure I am today shee was given you in marriage. You are   530
merrely disposed, said the Bridegroome, what thinke you I have
another wife? I thinke but as you speake, quoth the Gentleman,
for my daughter is below, and you say your wife is in the bed.
Below (said he) you are a merry man, and with that casting on
a night gowne, hee went downe, where when he saw his wife,   535
the Gentleman his Father, and a number of his friends assembled, hee was so confounded, that how to behave himselfe he
knew not; onely he cryde out that he was deceived. At this the
old woman arises, and making her selfe ignoraunt of all the
whole matter, inquires the cause of that sodayne tumult. When   540
she was told the new Bridegroome was founde in bed with her
daughter, she exclaimd against so great an injurie. Marian was
calde in quorum[1]: shee justified, it was by his allurement: he
being condemnd by all their consents, was adjudged unworthy
to have the Gentlewoman unto his Wife, and compeld (for   545
escaping of punishment) to marrie Marian: and the young
Gentleman (for his care in discovering the Farmers sonnes
lewdnes) was recompenst with the Gentlewomans ever during
love. |D2ᵛ|

Quoth *Lamilia*, and what of this? Nay nothing, said *Roberto*,   , 550
but that I have told you the effects of sodaine love: yet the best
is, my brother is a maidenly Batchler; and for your selfe, you
have not beene troubled with many suiters. The fewer the
better, said *Lucanio*. But brother, I con you little thanke for this
tale, heereafter I pray you use other table talke. Lets then end   555
talk, quoth *Lamilia*, and you (signior *Lucanio*) and I will go to
the Chesse.[2] To Chesse, said he, what meane you by that? It is

---

[1] *calde in quorum*] i.e., brought to account (lit., into the presence of
a judge or judges, *coram judice*). On the confusion *quorum—coram*, see
McKerrow, ed., *Nashe*, 4:98–99; *OED*.

[2] *go to the Chesse*] Cf. *Machiavel's Dog*, 1617, B1ᵛ: "But leaving
Cardes, lett's goe to dice awhile" (in F. Aydelotte, *Elizabethan Rogues and
Vagabonds* [1913; repr. 1967], 88n.). In early use, often *the chess* (*OED*).

a game, said she, that the first daunger is but a checke,[1] the
worst, the giving of a mate.[2] Well, said *Roberto*, that game yee
have beene at already then, for you checkt him first with your
beauty, and gave your selfe for mate to him by your bounty.
Thats wel taken brother, said *Lucanio*, so have we past our
game at Chesse. Wil ye play at Tables then, said she? I cannot,
quoth hee, for I can goe no further with my game, if I be once
taken.[3] Will ye play then at cards? I, said he, so it bee at one
and thirtie.[4] That fooles game, said she? Wele all to hazard, said
Roberto, and brother you shall make one for an houre or two:
content, quoth he. So to dice they went, and fortune so favored
Lucanio, that while they continued square play, hee was no
looser. Anone coosenage came about, and his Angels being
double winged,[5] flew clean from before him. *Lamilia* being the
winner, preparde a banquet; which finished, *Roberto* advisde his
brother to departe home, and to furnish himselfe with more
Crownes, least hee were outcrackt with new commers.[6]

Lucanio loath to be outcountenanst, followed his advise,
desiring him to attend his returne, which hee[7] before had determined unrequested: For as soone as his brothers backe was
turned, *Roberto* begins to recken with La-|D3ʳ|*milia*, to bee a

---

[1] *checke*] With a play on "taunt" or "reprimand."

[2] *giving of a mate*] i.e., checkmate (*OED*). The play on *mate* follows. If
a threatening sense (suggested by "the worst"), then *mate* = *adversary*
(*OED* 2), perhaps *rival*. Cf. G. Harvey, 1593 (ed. Grosart), 1:275: "if
kinges peradventure finde themselves somewhat shrewdly mated, alas we
poore subjectes must be content to be checked."

[3] *if . . . taken*] Lucanio probably means *captured* in love. Once
"taken" in backgammon a piece in fact goes *back* to the start.

[4] *one and thirtie*] Card game (sometimes *trentuno*) like black jack in
which the object was to get the closest to thirty-one points ("pips") in
three cards. Perhaps too simple to allow for cheating. But since another
name appears to have been "bone-ace" (Florio, 1611, *s.v. Trentuno*), an
allusion through *bone-ache* to venereal disease would explain Lamilia's
reluctance (cf. "Spanish pip"). Cf. *NDC*, 26; *DC-C*, 5: "Irish one and
thirtie."

[5] *Angels . . . winged*] The Archangel Michael, after which it is named,
shows both wings. Worth about ten shillings. Cf. *GMG*, 9:181.

[6] *outcrackt . . . commers*] i.e., outbid. *OED* gives "to make a louder crack
or noise than; to outbrag" with this the first and first for *new-comer*.

[7] *hee*] i.e., Roberto.

sharer as well in the money deceitfully wonne, as in the Dia- 580
mond so wilfully given. But she, *secundum mores meretricis*,
jested thus with the scholer. Why *Roberto*, are you so well read,
and yet shewe your selfe so shallow witted, to deeme women so
weake of conceit, that they see not into mens demerites. Suppose (to make you my stale to catch the woodcocke your broth- 585
er) that my tongue over-running myne intent, I spake of liberall
rewarde: but what I promist, theres the point;[1] at least what I
part with I will be well advisde.[2] It may be you will thus reason:
Had not *Roberto* traind *Lucanio* unto *Lamilias* lure, *Lucanio* had
not now beene *Lamilias* pray: therefore sith by *Roberto* she
possesseth the prize, *Roberto* merites an equal part. Monstrous 590
absurd if so you reason; as wel you may reason thus: *Lamilias*
dog hath kild her a Deere, therefore his Mistris must make him
a pastie. No, poore pennilesse Poet, thou art beguilde in mee,
and yet I wonder how thou couldst, thou hast beene so often
beguilde. But it fareth with licentious men, as with the chased 595
Bore in the stream, who being greatly refresht with swimming,
never feeleth anie smart untill hee perish recurelesly wounded
with his owne weapons.[3] Reasonlesse *Roberto*, that having but a
brokers place, askest a lenders reward. Faithles *Roberto*, that
hast attempted to betray thy brother, irreligiously forsaken thy 600
Wife, deservedly been in thy fathers eie an abject: thinkst thou
Lamilia so loose, to consort with one so lewd. No, hypocrite,
the sweet Gentleman thy brother, I will till death love, and thee
while I live, loath. This share *Lamilia* gives thee, other getst
thou none. 605

As *Roberto* would have replide, *Lucanio* approcht: |D3ᵛ| to
whom *Lamilia* discourst the whole deceipt of his brother, and
never rested intimating malitious arguments, til *Lucanio* utterly

---

[1] *what . . . point*] Cf. Tilley, P602; N272: "He that promises too
much means nothing."

[2] *will . . . advisde*] will have considered carefully.

[3] *chased . . . weapons*] Boars were great swimmers (see E. Topsell,
History of Four-Footed Beasts, 1607, 693ff.); but this characteristic I
cannot find. That the beaver castrates itself when pursued by hunters for
its stones (Pliny, *Hist. Nat.*, VIII.47) was frequently referred to; see, e.g.,
Nashe, 2:215. Is this fabricated to suggest the elaborate, fanciful
euphuisms associated with Greene?

refusde *Roberto* for his brother, and for ever forbad him his house. And when he would have yeelded reasons, and formed excuse, *Lucanios* impatience (urgd by her importunate malice) forbad all reasoning with them that were reasonlesse, and so giving him Jacke Drums intertainment,[1] shut him out of doores: whom we will follow, and leave *Lucanio* to the mercie of *Lamilia*. *Roberto* in an extreme extasie, rent his haire, curst his destenie, blamd his trechery, but most of all exclaimd against *Lamilia*: and in her against all enticing Curtizans, in these tearms.

What meant the Poets in invective verse,
To sing Medeas shame,[2] *and Scillas pride,*[3]
Calipsoes charmes,[4] *by which so many dyde?*
Onely for this their vices they rehearse,
That curious wits which in this world converse,[5]
May shun the dangers and enticing shoes,[6]
Of such false Syrens, those home-breeding foes,[7]
That from the eyes their venim do disperse.

---

[1] *Jack Drums intertainment*] A drum should be *beaten out of doors*. The joke became popular.

[2] Medeas shame] At falling in love with or bewitching Jason, bringing about many deaths. Greene quotes or paraphrases six times from Ovid, *Metamorphoses*, VII.18: "*Video meliora proboque, deteriora sequor*" (Applegate). Medea, Calipso, Circe, and Scylla occur together often with Greene.

[3] Scillas pride] For rejecting Glaucus. Circe, her rival in love, turned this water nymph into a monster with six heads which snatched sailors from passing ships. T. Lodge's *Scilla's Metamorphosis*, 1589 (ed. 1883), 1:28, has "Scylla's pride" in the stanza before "L'Envoy."

[4] Calipsoes charmes] The enchantress with whom Odysseus stayed seven years. She seems to have caused no deaths.

[5] converse] (1) dwell, (2) have sex (*OED* 2.b). Cf. *FrF*, 8:161: "converst dishonestly with *Isabel*"; 2 Peter 2:7.

[6] shoes] (shows) appearances. Phantasmal appearances may be intended (cf. "*which in this world converse*"), for which 1611 (*Cymb.*) is *OED*'s first (*Show* 11).

[7] home-breeding foes] i.e., foes *to* home-breeding (conjugal relations), playing on *home-bred*, meaning inexperienced, unsophisticated (which describes their victims).

> *So soone kils not the Basiliske with sight,*[1]
> *The Vipers tooth is not so venemous,*[2]
> *The Adders tung not halfe so dangerous,*[3]
> *As they that beare the shadow of delight,*   630
> *Who chaine blind youths in tramels of their haire,*[4]
> *Till wast bring woe, and sorrow hast despaire.*

With this he laid his head on his hand, and leant his elbow
on the earth, sighing out sadly,

> *Heu patior telis vulnera facta meis!*[5]   635

On the other side of the hedge sate one that heard his sor-
row: who getting over, came towards him, and |D4ʳ| brake off
his passion. When hee approached, hee saluted *Roberto* in this
sort.

Gentleman, quoth hee, (for so you seeme) I have by   640
chaunce heard you discourse some part of your greefe; which
appeareth to be more than you will discover, or I can conceipt.
But if you vouchsafe such simple comforte as my abilitie may
yeeld, assure your selfe, that I wil indevour to doe the best, that
either may procure you profite, or bring you pleasure: the   645
rather, for that I suppose you are a scholler, and pittie it is men
of learning should live in lacke.

Roberto wondring to heare such good wordes, for that this
iron age[6] affoordes few that esteeme of vertue; returnd him

---

[1] Basiliske ...] Supposed able to kill with its look. Wm. M. Carroll,
Animal Conventions (1954), 93, finds 22 in Greene.

[2] Vipers tooth ...] See note to "female serpents," line 209.

[3] Adders tung ...] Cf. S. Gosson, *School*, 1579, Bviijʳ (facs., 1973):
"Adders that sting with pleasure, and kil with paine."

[4] tramels ... haire] i.e., plaits. *Trammel*, a net used for catching birds
or fish. Greene uses the conceit so often that it might have been identified with him; in *NTL*, 8:14, 90, 93, 107; *FrF*, 8:178; *GMG*, 9:128, 149;
GV, 12:241. T. W. Baldwin discusses the image in Greene, in *Literary
Genetics* (1959), 89–91.

[5] Heu ... meis!] "Alas! I suffer wounds made by my own darts!"
(Ovid, *Heroides*, II.48).

[6] iron age] Commonplace for hard times (ultimately from Hesiod and
Ovid). Cf. *DC-C*, 12. On the identity of this Player-Patron, see Appendix
D.

650 thankfull gratulations,[1] and (urgde by necessitie) uttered his present griefe, beseeching his advise how he might be imployed. Why, easily, quoth hee, and greatly to your benefite: for men of my profession gette by schollers their whole living. What is your profession, said *Roberto?* Truly sir, saide hee, I am
655 a player. A player, quoth *Roberto,* I tooke you rather for a Gentleman of great living, for if by outward habit men should be censured,[2] I tell you, you would bee taken for a substantiall man. So am I where I dwell (quoth the player) reputed able at my proper cost to build a Windmill. What though the world
660 once went hard with me, when I was faine to carry my playing Fardle a footebacke[3]; *Tempora mutantur,*[4] I know you know the meaning of it better than I, but I thus conster it, its otherwise now; for my very share in playing apparell will not be sold for two hundred pounds.[5] Truly (said *Roberto*) tis straunge, that you
665 should so prosper in that vayne practise, for that it seemes to mee your voice is nothing |D4ᵛ| gratious. Nay then, saide the Player, I mislike your judgement: why, I am as famous for Delphrigus,[6] and the King of Fairies,[7] as ever was any of my

---

[1] *gratulations*] expressions of thanks (*OED* 3, citing this), or compliments. But perhaps of joy or greeting (*OED* 2, 4), since we have "thankfull." Apparently a Greene favorite, it suggested the pretentiously academic; cf. *Cobbler of Canterbury,* 1590 (1987), 45: "the wily wench hearing such a Schollerlike gratulation, seeing by this salute, that Schollers had read of Love, more then they coulde say of Love...."

[2] *if... censured*] From John 7:24: "Judge not according to the utter aperaunce."

[3] *Fardle a footebacke*] bundle on (my) back (as I walked). A "humorous formation after *horseback*" (*OED*), presumably original with Nashe in preface to *Menaphon,* 1589, 3:324.

[4] Tempora mutantur] Cf. *Penelope's Web,* 5:188: "*Tempora mutantur, et nos mutamur in illis.*" Bond (ed., *Lyly,* 1:360) says it is medieval. *K-HD,* 16, has "the times are changed, and men are changed in the times."

[5] *apparell... pounds*] This seems exaggerated. For examples of costs of wardrobes, see E. K. Chambers, *Elizabethan Stage,* 1:372, and Mary Edmond, *RES* 25 (1974): 9. Chambers apparently saw no exaggeration here (1:349); Alwin Thaler did, in *Studies in Philology* 15 (1918): 95.

[6] *Delphrigus*] Probably the hero of some lost dramatized chivalric romance. Phrygia was Troy. *Common Conditions* (ent. 1574) has a duke of Phrygia and scenes laid there. For a "Phrygio" see John Marston, *Scourge of Villany,* VIII.122 (1598, ed. Davenport), and E. Guilpin, *Skialetheia,*

time. The twelve labors of Hercules have I terribly thundred on
the Stage,[1] and plaid three Scenes of the Devill in the High way   670
to heaven.[2] Have ye so (saide *Roberto?*) then I pray you pardon
me. Nay more (quoth the Player) I can serve to make a pretie
speech, for I was a countrey Author, passing at a Morrall, for
twas I that pende the Morrall of mans witte,[3] the Dialogue of
Dives,[4] and for seven yeers space[5] was absolute Interpreter to   675
the puppets. But now my Almanacke is out of date:[6]

> *The people make no estimation,*
> *Of Morrals teaching education.*[7]

Was not this prettie for a plaine rime extempore? if ye will ye
shall have more. Nay its enough, said *Roberto,* but how meane   680
you to use mee? Why sir, in making Playes, said the other, for

---

III.86 (1598, ed. Carroll), both of whom may be Thomas Lodge. Alfred
Harbage and S. Schoenbaum list the Player's plays as addenda to the
year 1570, in *Annals of English Drama, 975–1700* (1964), 40.

[7] *King of Fairies*] Perhaps a reference to *Huon of Bordeaux,* performed
as an old play at the Rose in 1593.

[1] *twelve . . . Hercules . . .*] Always popular. Chambers quotes (*Elizabethan Stage,* 2:90 and n.) from a description of a performance before the
Earl of Lincoln in 1572 which has "the Antiques of carying of men one
uppon an other which som men call *labores Herculis.*" The rant (Bottom's
"Ercles' vein") is frequently referred to.

[2] *three Scenes . . . heaven*] Unidentified. A late morality or moral
interlude.

[3] *Morrall of mans witte*] Any of several moral interludes which present
Wit entering into manhood. One, *Marriage of Wit and Wisdom* (attr. to
Francis Merbury, MS. either 1570 or 1579), is the title given by the
players in *Sir Thomas More,* though they perform an altered version of a
scene from *Lusty Juventus.*

[4] *Dialogue of Dives*] scriptural comedy, now lost, based on parable of
the rich man and the beggar. The players in *More* offer "dives and Lazarus," and Owlet's company in *Histriomastix* "The Devil and Dives."

[5] *seven yeers space*] i.e., the length of an apprenticeship.

[6] *my . . . date*] i.e., "people have got tired of me, my performance—
that of an actor of moralities—is no longer in fashion." So McKerrow on
Pierce, 1592, *Nashe,* 1:167.

[7] *The people . . .*] Recalling W. Webbe's *Discourse of English Poetry,*
1586 (*Elizabethan Critical Essays,* ed. Smith, 1:294): "Those verses which
be made Extempore are of no great estimation: those which are unartificiall are utterly repelled as too foolish."

which you shall be well paid, if you will take the paines.

Roberto perceiving no remedie, thought best in respect of his present necessitie, to try his wit, and went with him willingly:
685 who lodgd him at the Townes end in a house of retayle,[1] where what happened our Poet, you shall after heare. There by conversing with bad company, he grew *A malo in peius*,[2] falling from one vice to an other: and so having founde a vaine to finger crowns,[3] he grew cranker than *Lucanio*, who by this time be-
690 gan to droope, being thus dealt with by *Lamilia*. Shee having bewitched him with hir enticing wiles, caused him to consume in lesse than two yeeres that infinite treasure gathered by his father with so many a poore mans curse. His lands sold, his jewels pawnd, his money wasted, he |E1^r| was casseerd by
695 *Lamilia*, that had coossend him of all. Then walkt he like one of Duke *Humfreys* Squires,[4] in a thread-bare cloake, his hose drawne out with his heeles, his shooes unseamed, least his feete should sweate with heat: now (as witlesse as hee was) he remembred his Fathers words, his unkindnes to his brother, his
700 carelesnes of himselfe. In this sorrow he sate down on pennilesse bench;[5] where when *Opus* and *Usus*[6] told him by the

---

[1] *house of retayle*] Cf. *Nashe*, 2:149; *Disput.*, 41; *K-HD*, 40, of brothels: "Is it not great shame, that the houses of retaylers neare the Townes end, should be by their [the plays'] continuance impoverished?"

[2] A malo in peius] Cf. Stubbes, *Anatomy*, 1583, Fiij^v (facs., 1973): "*a malo, ad peius*, (as they say) from one mischiefe to an other." *GV* (12:206 and Q) has "*Malo in penis*"!

[3] *vaine . . . crowns*] Implying through unworthy means. Cf. *3C-C*, 32.

[4] *one . . . Squires*] i.e., poor and hungry. Originally those who loitered in the aisle of St. Paul's called "Duke Humphrey's Walk" (see McKerrow on *Pierce*, 1592, *Nashe*, 1:163), especially at dinner time, because they had no means to procure a meal. *ODEP*, 188, gives 1591 first (*Nashe*, 3:393). Cf. *Disput.*, 38.

[5] *sate . . . bench*] Proverbial for extreme poverty. R. Nares said a seat by this name was under a wooden canopy at the east end of old Carfax Church (*Glossary of Words, Phrases*, etc. [1905]). They must have been common. See E. H. Sugden, *Topographical Dictionary* (1925; repr. 1969), 402. Cf. *James IV*, IV.iii.32 (ed. Sanders).

[6] Opus *and* Usus] i.e., need. Schoolboy humor based on Lyly's Grammar, *Shorte Intro.*, 1574, Dvj^r (ed. Blach, *Shakespeare Jahrbuch* 45 [1909]: 63): "*Opus* and *usus*, when they be latine for neede, require an ablative case." Cf. *Pierce*, 1592, *Nashe*, 1:161; Harvey, *FL*, 56; *First Part*

chymes in his stomacke[1] it was time to fall unto meat, he was
faine with the Camelion to feed upon the aire,[2] and make patience his best repast.

    While he was at this feast, *Lamilia* came flaunting by, gar-   705
nished with the jewels wherof she beguiled him, which sight
served to close his stomacke after his cold cheare.[3] *Roberto*
hearing of his brothers beggery, albeit he had little remorse of
his miserable state, yet did seeke him out, to use him as a
propertie,[4] whereby *Lucanio* was somewhat provided for. But   710
beeing of simple nature, hee served but for a blocke to whet
Robertoes wit on:[5] which the poore foole perceiving, he forsooke
all other hopes of life,[6] and fell to be a notorious Pandar, in
which detested course he continued till death. But *Roberto* now
famozed for an Arch-plaimaking-poet, his purse like the sea   715
somtime sweld, anon like the same sea fell to a low ebbe; yet
seldom he wanted, his labors were so well esteemed. Marry this
rule he kept, what ever he fingerd afore hand, was the certaine
meanes to unbinde a bargaine, and being askt why hee so
slightly[7] dealt with them that did him good? It becoms me, saith   720
hee, to bee contrary to the worlde; for commonly when vulgar
men receive earnest, they doo performe, when I am paid any

... *Parnassus*, line 210 (ed. Leishman), 146.

  [1] *by ... stomacke*] Cf. *K-HD*, 65: "by the chimes in his belly."

  [2] *Camelion ... aire*] Cf. Tilley, M226: "A Man cannot live on air
(like a chameleon)"; Greene, *Royal Exchange*, 1590, 7:230; *FrF*, 8:180.

  [3] *to close ... cheare*] i.e., to fill up his stomach (to "top it out"), used
ironically, after his poor meal. Cf. *The Shrew*, V.ii.9–10: "My banket is
to close our stomachs up / After our great good cheer."

  [4] *propertie*] i.e., "a mere means to an end, an instrument," presumably (*OED* 5, 1598), perhaps to supply dupes. Cf. *Piers*, 157: "albeit he
used Ursula his daughter as a propertie to inthrall yong Gentlemen, as
hee had earst done Flavius."

  [5] *blocke ... on*] whetstone (*OED* 13, citing this only). *Block* was a
term for the stupid (1.b).

  [6] *forsooke ... life*] Nashe uses this expression in *Menaphon*, 1589, 3:316.

  [7] *slightly*] craftily (to deceive). Perhaps *sleightly* (as defined in *OED*),
which spelling, Cobb notes, appears in sequent Qq.

thing afore-hand, I breake my promise.[1] |E1^v| He had shift of
lodgings, where in every place his Hostesse writ up the wofull
725   remembrance of him, his laundresse, and his boy;[2] for they were
ever his in houshold, beside retainers in sundry other places.
His companie were lightly the lewdest persons in the land, apt
for pilferie, perjurie, forgerie, or any villainy.[3] Of these hee knew
the casts to cog at cards,[4] coossen at Dice[5]; by these he learnd
730   the legerdemaines of nips, foystes,[6] connycatchers,[7] crosbyters,[8]

---

[1] *when . . . promise*] E. H. Miller (*Philological Quarterly* 33 [1954]:
359) thinks Greene acknowledges here with pride the simultaneous sale
of *Orlando Furioso* to rival dramatic companies, which he is accused of by
"Cuthbert Connycatcher" in *DC-C*, 37.

[2] *laundresse . . . boy*] Laundresses were generally regarded as of dubious
virtue. Perhaps a reference to his mistress Em Ball and son by her.

[3] *apt for pilferie . . . .*] H. Crosse, *Virtue's Commonwealth*, 1603 (ed.
1878), 117, quotes from here. What follows are categories of crimes and
criminals in the cant that Greene, claiming special knowledge, discusses
in a series we call cony-catching pamphlets, of late 1591 and early 1592.
This is, in effect, an advertisement. These tracts established a vogue
which lasted about twenty-five years: *Notable Discovery of Cozenage* (ent.
S.R. 13 Dec. 1591), *Second Part of Cony-Catching* (S.R. 13 Dec. 1591),
Third and Last Part of Cony-Catching (S.R. 7 Feb. 1592), *Disputation
Between a He Cony-Catcher and a She Cony-Catcher* (not ent., earliest ed.
1592), and *Black Book's Messenger* (S.R. 21 Aug. 1592). Greene de-
scribes his relationship with "those mad fellowes" in *NDC*, 7–15. The
terms here seem drawn from the first two. On this literature and
Greene's part in it, see F. Aydelotte, *Eliz. Rogues and Vagabonds* (1913;
repr. 1967), A. V. Judges, *Eliz. Underworld* (1930; repr. 1965), and J. A.
S. McPeek, *The Black Book of Knaves and Unthrifts* (1969).

[4] *casts . . . cards*] i.e., the tricks to cheat. *OED* assumes that *cog* here
is transferred from its old, typical use with dice, though there was a
general "to deceive, cheat" (*OED* 3). The Art of Cony-Catching, in
NDC, is specifically cheating at cards. Cf. "cast at cards" in *2C-C*, 26.

[5] *coossen at Dice*] i.e., to cheat. Generally supposed, on slight evidence, originally to have implied "under pretext of cousinship" (*OED*).
Greene mentions but refuses to describe dice tricks (*NDC*, 38). They
were fully described in *A Manifest Detection of the Most Vile and Detestable
Use of Diceplay* (1552 or earlier), a book he relied on.

[6] *nips, foystes*] cutpurses, pickpockets. Their activities are illustrated
in *2C-C*, 29–43. *3C-C*, 36, and *Disput.*, 12, mention the "Leger de
maine" necessary in a foist.

lifts,[1] high Lawyers,[2] and all the rabble of that uncleane generation of vipers:[3] and pithily could he paint out their whole courses
of craft: So cunning he was in all craftes, as nothing rested in
him almost but craftines. How often the Gentlewoman his Wife
labored vainely to recall him, is lamentable to note: but as one 735
given over to all lewdnes, he communicated her sorrowfull lines
among his loose truls, that jested at her bootlesse laments. If he
could any way get credite on scores, he would then brag his
creditors carried stones, comparing every round circle to a
groning O procured by a painfull burden.[4] The shamefull ende 740
of sundry his consorts deservedly punished for their amisse,
wrought no compunction in his heart: of which one, brother to

---

[7] *connycatchers*] thieves and sharpers. These took advantage of the
innocence of their dupes—conies, usually countrymen. "A term made
famous by Greene" (*OED*, with the title *NDC* first), used by him to
cover the whole art of cozenage, though he also has a "Conny-catching
Law" in *NDC* to describe cheating at cards (17–37), the same described
in *Manifest Detection* (1552) as Barnard's Law.

[8] *crosbyters*] Second of two "Arts" in *NDC*. Though sometimes to
cheat in general, *crossbite* usually suggested "in return," as in the epistle
to *NDC*, which adds a special sense, probably here: "I meane not Cros
biters at dice [etc.]. . . . But I meane a more dishonourable Arte, when a
base Roague, eyther keepeth a whore as his friende, or marries one to be
his mainteyner, and with her not onely cros-bites men of good calling,
but especially poore ignoraunt countrey Farmers" (14–15).

[1] *lifts*] "he that stealeth any parcels, and slily taketh them away" (*2C-
C*, 8—first in *OED* for *sb.*). Cf. *2C-C*, 44–47: "Lifting Law."

[2] *high Lawyers*] highwaymen, chief participants "in high Lawe," in
NDC, 38.

[3] *generation of vipers*] Cf. Matt. 3:7, 12:34, 23:33, Luke 3:7. Commonplace in threats to the community—young vipers eat their way out
of their mother's wombs; females in sex bite off the heads of males; cf.
1H6, III.i.72–73; see J. Lat. Simmons, *Shakespeare Quarterly* 27 (1976):
329–32. Frequent in Greene.

[4] *carried . . . burden*] Referring to ale-house charges. Cf. *DC-C*, 38:
"These *Souldados* . . . have shewed theyr Rithmetike with chalke on every
post in the house, figured in Cyphers like round Os, till they make the
goodman cry O, O, O." See Hoy, 4:132; S. R.'s *Greene's Ghost*, 1602
(1623, ed. 1860), 31: "leaving an Alewife in the lurch, is termed making
her carie stones." A "great round *O* [stands] for a Shilling" (1656, in
Jonson [ed. Herford and Simpson], 10:306).

a Brothell hee kept, was trust under a tree as round as a Ball.[1]

To some of his swearing companions thus it happened:[2] A
745 crue of them sitting in a Taverne carowsing, it fortuned an
honest Gentleman and his friend, to enter their roome: some of
them beeing acquainted with him, in their domineering drunk-
en vaine would have no nay but downe hee must needes sitte
with them; beeing placed, no remedie there was, but he must
750 needes keepe even compasse[3] with their unseemely carowsing.
|E2ʳ| Which he refusing, they fell from high words to sound
strokes, so that with much adoo the Gentleman saved his owne,[4]
and shifted from their company. Being gone, one of these
tiplers forsooth lackt a gold Ring, the other sware[5] they saw the
755 Gentleman take it from his hande. Upon this the Gentleman
was indited before a Judge, these honest men are deposde:
whose wisedome[6] weighing the time of the braule, gave light to
the Jury, what power wine-washing poyson[7] had, they according
unto conscience found the Gentleman not guiltie, and God
760 released by that verdit the innocent.

With his accusers thus it fared: One of them for murder was
worthily executed: the other never since prospered: the third,

---

[1] *one . . . Ball*] Alluding to the hanging at Tyborn of Cutting Ball, a
thief whose sister Em seems to have been Greene's mistress. Not to be
confused with *Bull*, the hangman, to whom Lawrence, in *2C-C*, 36, and
Disput., 30, is "brother in law." *as . . . Ball*, i.e., quickly. Cf. Stubbes,
Anatomy, 1583 (facs., 1973), Kvijᵛ; W. Vaughan, *Golden Grove*, 1608 (in
McKerrow, ed., *Nashe*, 4:231), of the principal demanded by a usurer:
"whensoever this reprobate cut-throate demaundeth it, then presently as
round as a ball, he commenceth his statute-marchant against him."

[2] *To some . . . .*] This episode may have been recognizable to contemporaries. C. Collins (ed., *Plays & Poems*, 1:9 n.) thought something
dropped. To Cobb (clxxxix) it must have autobiographical significance
for Greene.

[3] *keepe even compasse*] Etiquette required that a toast be returned.

[4] *saved his owne*] i.e., "skin," presumably, though earliest for the
phrase in *OED* is 1642.

[5] *sware*] Probably archaic past of *swear*, a form *OED* records.

[6] *whose wisedome*] i.e., the judge's. The "honest men" would be the
"honest Gentleman and his friend" of above.

[7] *wine-washing poyson*] Cf. *Vinum quasi venenum* (see McKerrow, ed.,
Nashe, 4:434).

sitting not long after upon a lustie horse, the beast sodenly
dyde under him, God amend the man.

Roberto every day acquainted with these examples, was notwithstanding nothing bettered, but rather hardened in wickednesse.[1] At last was that place justified,[2] God warneth men by
dreams and visions in the night, and by knowne examples in
the day, but if hee returne not, hee comes uppon him with
judgement that shall bee felt. For now when the number of
deceites caused Roberto to bee hatefull almost to all men, his
immeasurable drinking had made him the perfect Image of the
dropsie,[3] and the loathsome scourge of Lust tyrannized in his
bones: lying in extreame poverty, and having nothing to pay
but chalke,[4] which now his Host accepted not for currant, this
miserable man lay comfortlesly languishing, having but one
groat left (the just proportion of his Fathers Legacie) which
looking on, he cryed: O now it is too late, too late to buy witte
with thee: and therefore |E2ᵛ| will I see if I can sell to carelesse
youth what I negligently forgot to buy.

Heere (Gentlemen) breake I off Robertoes speach; whose life
in most parts agreeing with mine, found one selfe punishment
as I have doone. Heereafter suppose me the saide Roberto, and
I will goe on with that hee promised: Greene will send you now
his groats-worth of wit, that never shewed a mites-worth in his
life: and though no man now bee by to doo me good: yet ere I
die I will by my repentaunce indevour to doo all men good.

> Deceiving world,[5] that with alluring toyes,
> Hast made my life the subject of thy scorne:

---

[1] *hardened in wickedness*] Recalling *Consuetudo peccandi, tollit sensum peccati*, which is in *NTL*, 8:101, *GMG*, 9:180, and *Repent.*, 10.

[2] *justified*] confirmed. The "place" is Matt. 2:12. Cf. also Gen. 46:2, Dan. 7:2, 7, 2:19, Acts 16:9, 18:9.

[3] *dropsie*] *FrF*, 8:140: "He that hath the dropsie, drinketh while he bursteth, and yet not satisfied." On the cause of Greene's death, see Introduction, n. 60.

[4] *chalke*] i.e., on credit; see note to "carried ... burden," line 740. Cf. *GMG*, 9:181 (in the brothel).

[5] Deceiving world] Cf. Litany in *Book of Common Prayer* (1559): "frome all the deceiptes of the worlde, the Fleshe and the Devill. *Good Lorde delyver us.*"

790 *And scornest now to lend thy fading joyes,*
To length my life, whom friends have left forlorne.
How well are they that die ere they be borne,
    And never see thy sleights, which few men shun,
    Till unawares they helpelesse are undone.

795 *Oft have I sung of Love, and of his fire,*
But now I finde that Poet was advizde;
Which made full feasts increasers of desire,[1]
And proves weake love was with the poore despizde.
For when the life with food is not suffizde,
800   *What thought of Love; what motion of delight;*
    What pleasance can proceed from such a wight?

Witnesse my want, the murderer of my wit;
My ravisht sence of wonted furie reft;[2]
Wants such conceit, as should in Poems fit,
805 *Set downe the sorrow wherein I am left:* |E3ʳ|
But therefore have high heavens their gifts bereft:
    Because so long they lent them mee to use,
    And I so long their bountie did abuse.

O that a yeare were graunted me to live,
810 *And for that yeare my former wits restorde:*
What rules of life, what counsell would I give?
How should my sinne with sorrow be deplorde?
But I must die of every man abhorde.
    Time loosely spent will not againe be wonne,
815   *My time is loosely spent, and I undone.*

O horrenda fames, how terrible are thy assaults! but *vermis
conscientiae,* more wounding are thy stings. Ah Gentlemen, that
live to read my broken and confused lines, looke not I should
(as I was wont) delight you with vaine fantasies, but gather my
820 follies altogether; and as yee would deale with so many parricides,

---

[1] that Poet ...] Terence. Greene twice quotes "*Sine Cerere et baco
[Baccho] friget Venus*" (9:335; 12:91), attributing it to "the olde Poet";
from *Eunuchus,* line 732 (IV.v.6; Applegate).
    [2] murderer ... reft] Cf. Tilley, 450: "A poet in adversity can hardly
make verses."

cast them into the fire: call them *Telegones*, for now they kil
their Father,[1] and every lewd line in them written, is a deepe
piercing wound to my heart; every idle houre spent by any in
reading them, brings a million of sorrowes to my soule. O that
the teares of a miserable man (for never any man was yet more
miserable) might wash their memorie out with my death; and
that those works with mee together might bee interd. But sith
they cannot, let this my last worke witnes against them with
mee, how I detest them. Blacke is the remembrance of my
blacke workes, blacker than night, blacker than death, blacker
than hell.

Learne wit by my repentance (Gentlemen) and let these few
rules following be regarded in your lives. |E3ᵛ|

1 First in al your actions set God before your eies;[2] for the
  feare of the Lord is the beginning of wisdome:[3] Let his word
  be a lanterne to your feet, and a light unto your paths,[4]
  then shall you stand as firme rocks, and not be moved.[5]
2 Beware of looking backe,[6] for God will not bee mocked;[7]
  and of him that hath received much, much shal be demaunded.[8]

---

[1] Telegones . . . *Father*] Son of Odysseus and Circe who unknowingly
killed his father. In *Tristia*, I.i.114, Ovid calls his books on love
"Telegoni," suggesting that they were responsible for his troubles.
Greene thought of himself, as did others, as an Ovid; see *GMG*, 9:121;
GV, 12:274; G. Harvey, *Pierce's Supererogation*, 1593 (ed. Grosart), 2:94.
Telegone is singular in *Orlando* (line 65)—an "extraordinary mistake" (W.
W. Greg, *Two Elizabethan Stage Abridgements* [1922], 204, 284). Greene
has a character called Telegonus in *Alcida*.

[2] *set . . . eies*] Cf. Ps. 16:8, 36:1, 54:3, 86:14. Listed precepts occur in
FrF, *GMG*, *Black Book's Messenger*, *Repent*.

[3] *feare . . . wisdome*] From Ps. 111:10 and Prov. 9:10. Quoted in
Repent., 29.

[4] *Let . . . paths*] From Ps. 119:105. Cf. *Repent.*, 30.

[5] *as . . . moved*] Cf. Matt. 7:24, Ps. 27:5, and, for "not be moved,"
Ps. 62:2, 6.

[6] *Beware . . . backe*] From Luke 9:62: "No man havyng put his hande
to the plowe, and lookynge backe, is apt to the kyngdome of God."

[7] *God . . . mocked*] From Gal. 6:7 (Coverdale: "God wil not be
mocked").

[8] *of him . . . demaunded*] From Luke 12:48.

3 If thou be single, and canst abstain,[1] turne thy eies from vanitie;[2] for there is a kinde of women bearing the faces of Angels, but the hearts of Devils,[3] able to intrap the elect if it were possible.[4]

845 4 If thou bee married, forsake not the wife of thy youth to follow straunge flesh; for whoremongers and adulterers the Lord will judge. The doore of a harlot leadeth downe to death, and in her lips there dwels destruction; her face is decked with odors, but she bringeth a man to a morsell of 850 bread and nakednes: of which my selfe am instance.[5]

5 If thou be left rich, remember those that want, and so deale, that by thy wilfulnes thy selfe want not: Let not Taverners and Victuallers be thy Executors; for they will bring thee to a dishonorable grave.[6]

855 6 Oppresse no man; for the crie of the wronged ascendeth to the eares of the Lord:[7] neyther delight to increase by Usurie,[8] least thou loose thy habitation in the everlasting Tabernacle.

7 Beware of building thy house to thy neighbors hurt; for the stones will crie to the timber; Wee were laid together in

---

[1] *canst abstain*] Places here and following recall 1 Cor. 7:9–10.

[2] *turne . . . vanitie*] From Ps. 119:37.

[3] *faces . . . Devils*] This may recall *Anatomy*, 1589, *Nashe*, 1:13: "I meane . . . to let an Author of late memorie be my speaker, who affyrmeth that they carrie Angels in their faces to entangle men and devils in their devices." McKerrow cannot identify the author certainly, but cites (4:16) Gascoigne's epilogue to *Steel Glass*, 1577: "With Angels face, and harmefull helish harts," and a place in *Courtier*.

[4] *to intrap . . . possible*] From Mark 13:22 (Genevan): "For false Christs shal rise . . . to deceive if it were possible, the very elect."

[5] *If thou bee married . . . .*] Assembled from Prov. 5:18, 6:24, Hebr. 13:4, Prov. 7:21, 27, 6:26 (Genevan). Greene paraphrases Prov. 5:3–5 in *NDC*, 43; *Repent.*, 21, gives a similar passage. He quotes almost verbatim Genevan Prov. 6:24–33 in *NTL*, 8:80–81; "wife of thy youth" occurs in *FrF*, 8:116, 140, 166.

[6] *Let not . . . grave*] Cf. *Quip* (facs., 1954), H2^r: "hee is borne to make the Tavernes ritch and himselfe a begger."

[7] *Oppresse . . . Lord*] Suggests 2 Sam. 22:7, Ps. 34:15, James 5:4.

[8] *neyther . . . Usurie*] Cf. Ezek. 18:8, 13, 17.

bloud[1]: and those that so erect houses, calling them by their 860
names,[2] shall lie in the grave lyke sheepe, and death shall
gnaw upon their soules.[3] |E4ʳ|

8 If thou be poore, be also patient, and strive not to grow rich
by indirect meanes; for goods so gotten shal vanish like
smoke.[4]   865

9 If thou bee a Father, Maister, or Teacher, joyne good example with good counsaile; else little availe precepts, where
life is different.

10 If thou be a Sonne or Servant, despise not reproofe;[5] for
though correction bee bitter at the first, it bringeth pleasure 870
in the end.

Had I regarded the first of these rules, or beene obedient to
the last; I had not now at my last ende, beene left thus deso-
late. But now, though to my selfe I give *Consilium post facta*; yet
to others they may serve for timely precepts. And therefore 875
(while life gives leave) I will send warning to my olde consorts,
which have lived as loosely as my selfe, albeit weaknesse will
scarse suffer me to write, yet to my fellow Schollers about this
Cittie, will I direct these few insuing lines.

---

[1] *Beware ... in bloud*] Based on Jer. 22:13: "Woe worth him that
buildeth his house with unryghteousnesse, and his parlours with the good
that he hath gotten by violence, whiche never recompenceth his
neyghbours labour, nor payeth hym his hyre," with Genevan gloss "By
bribes and extorsion," which Nashe uses in *Christ's Tears*, 1593, 2:93.
Cf. also Hab. 2:8–12, esp. 11–12, with the Genevan gloss.

[2] *calling ... names*] Based on Ps. 49:11: "yet they thinke ... that
their dwellyng places shal endure from one generation to another, and
cal the landes after their owne names."

[3] *shall lie ... soules*] From Ps. 49:14 (Genevan): "Like shepe thei lie
in grave: death devoureth them [Coverdale: 'shal gnawe upon them']."

[4] *shal ... smoke*] Cf. Isaiah 51:6.

[5] *despise not reproofe*] Based on Prov. 1:25.

To those Gentlemen his Quondam acquaintance,
that spend their wits in making plaies, R. G.
wisheth a better exercise, and wisdome
to prevent his extremities.[1]

885

890

895

If wofull experience may move you (Gentlemen) to beware,
or unheard of wretchednes intreate you to take heed: I doubt
not but you wil looke backe with sorrow on your time past, and
indevour with repentance to spend that which is to come.
Wonder not, (for with thee wil I first begin) thou famous gracer
of Tragedians, that *Greene*, who hath said with thee (like the
foole in his heart) There is no God,[2] shoulde now give |E4^v|
glorie unto his greatnes:[3] for penetrating is his power, his hand
lyes heavie upon me,[4] hee hath spoken unto mee with a voice of
thunder,[5] and I have felt he is a God that can punish enemies.[6]
Why should thy excellent wit, his gift, bee so blinded,[7] that thou
shouldst give no glorie to the giver? Is it pestilent Machivilian
pollicy[8] that thou hast studied? O peevish[9] follie! What are his

---

[1] To those Gentlemen. . . .] M. C. Bradbrook notes that letters urging
repentance on companions in former sins were an exercise in upper
school (*Shakespeare: The Poet and His World* [1978], 47), citing Erasmus,
De Conscrib. Epist., chap. x. H. Crosse, *Virtue's Commonwealth*, 1603
(1878), 122, gives a synopsis of this letter.

[2] *who . . . God*] From Ps. 14:1. On the Marlowe section of this letter
see Appendix E.

[3] *give . . . greatnes*] Cf., among other places, 1 Sam. 6:5.

[4] *his hand . . . me*] Cf. 1 Sam. 5:6. This address reflects Chaps. 5 and
6 of Samuel, of the plague visited against the men of Ashdod. Note the
Genevan margin.

[5] *voice of thunder*] Cf. Job 40:4, Ps. 77:18, 104:7, Rev. 14:2; *Nashe*,
1593, 2:121 (of atheism): "Who heareth the thunder, that thinkes not of
God?"; and S. Patericke's trans. of Gentillet, in *Discourse Upon the Means*
(1602), 95, of Caligula's fear of thunder.

[6] *I have . . . enemies*] Cf. Gentillet, in Patericke's trans. (*Discourse*
[1602], 92–93), on atheism.

[7] *wit . . . blinded*] Based on Deut. 16:19: "for gyftes do blynde the
eyes of the wise, and pervert the wordes of the ryghteous."

[8] *pollicy*] unscrupulous cunning. Perhaps suggested by its heavy use
in *Jew*. To N. W. Bawcutt, in *ELR* 1 (1971): 209, Greene "is not
twisting a previously innocent word into a new meaning, but rather
seeing Machiavellianism as the newest and most extreme form of the

rules but meere confused mockeries, able to extirpate in small time the generation of mankind. For if *Sic volo, sic iubeo*,[1] hold in those that are able to commaund: and if it be lawfull *Fas et nefas*[2] to do any thing that is beneficiall;[3] onely Tyrants should possesse the earth,[4] and they striving to exceed in tyrannie, should each to other be a slaughter man;[5] till the mightiest outliving all, one stroke were lefte for Death, that in one age mans life should end. The brocher[6] of this Diabolicall Atheisme is dead, and in his life had never the felicitie hee aymed at: but as he began in craft; lived in feare, and ended in despaire. *Quam inscrutabilia sunt Dei iudicia!*[7] This murderer of many brethren, had his conscience seared like *Caine*:[8] this betrayer of

900

905

---

patterns of evil behavior [already] suggested by the word."

[9] *peevish*] Other Qq have *punish*; Dyce suggested *brutish* (ed., *Dramatic Works* [1831], lxxix).

[1] Sic volo, sic iubeo] "As I wish, so I command." From Juvenal, *Satires*, VI.223, a misquotation of *hoc volo, sic iubeo*. It appears, as here, in *Tell-Troth's New-Year's Gift* (1593), 7; *Ratsey's Ghost* (1605), D4^r (facs., 1932).

[2] Fas et nefas] "by fair means or foul." J. C. Maxwell (*N&Q* 192 [1947]: 428), emending Lodge and Greene's *Looking Glass* (line 148, ed. Collins, 1:149), cites Horace, *Odes*, I.xviii.11–12: "*cum fas atque nefas exiguo.*" Cf. "*Sit fas aut nefas*" in *Titus*, II.i.133, for which J. W. Cunliffe suggested memories of Seneca's *Hippolytus*, *c.* line 1180 (*Influence of Seneca* [1893], 128). C. M. Ingleby (*Shakspere Allusion-Books* [1874], 1:viii) thought *GGW* here "perfectly reproduced" in Ulysses' "degree" speech (*Troi.*, I.iii.119–24). R. Lamson and H. Smith (*Renaissance England: Poetry and Prose* [1942], 426 n.) supply *per omne* ("By any means, good or bad"). Cf. the expression by Hand D of *More*, thought to be Shakespeare's, in Addition II, lines 202–10 (ed. Greg [1911], 76).

[3] *beneficiall*] i.e., to oneself.

[4] *Tyrants . . . earth*] i.e., and not the meek, of Matt. 5:5

[5] *slaughter man*] executioner. J. M. Robertson (*Shakespeare Canon* [1922], 26) thinks this (as one) word a favorite with Marlowe.

[6] *brocher*] i.e., broacher. Other Qq have *brother*. On Malone's misinterpretation and on Machiavelli, see Appendix E, n. 17.

[7] Quam . . . iudicia!] Based on Rom. 11:33 (Vulgate, but see Genevan and Bishops'). Cf. 1 Tim. 3:16; *Repent.*, 27; *Black Book's Messenger*, 32.

[8] *conscience . . . Caine*] Based on 1 Tim. 4:2; Gen. 4:15 (Genevan). Cf. *2C-C*, 6.

him that gave his life for him, inherited the portion of *Judas:*[1]
this Apostata perished as ill as *Julian:*[2] and wilt thou my friend
be his disciple? Looke but to me, by him perswaded to that
libertie,[3] and thou shalt find it an infernall bondage. I knowe the
least of my demerits merit this miserable death, but wilfull
striving against knowne truth, exceedeth all the terrors of my
soule.[4] Defer not[5] (with me) till this last point of extremitie;
for litle knowst thou how in the end thou shalt be visited.

With thee I joyne yong *Juvenall*,[6] that byting Satyrist, that
lastly[7] with mee together writ a Comedie.[8] |F1ʳ| Sweet boy,
might I advise thee, be advisde, and get not many enemies by
bitter wordes: inveigh against vaine men, for thou canst do it, no
man better, no man so well: thou hast a libertie to reproove all,
and name none; for one being spoken to, all are offended; none

---

[1] *portion of* Judas] i.e., suicide.

[2] *Apostata . . .* Julian] Roman emperor (332–363) famous for apostasy
("the Apostate") Cf. *Nashe*, 1593, 2:115: "In the very houre of death, to
Atheisticall *Julian* (who mockingly called all Christians *Gallileans*) appeared a grizly shaggy-bodied devill, who for all (at his sight) hee recant-
ingly cryed out. *Vicisti, Galilaee, vicisti....*" G. Harvey, 1593 (ed.
Grosart), 1:289, compares Greene with Julian.

[3] *libertie*] unrestrained conduct, in action, appetite or expression
(*OED*). Cf. *Piers*, 154: "libertie of unbrideled appetite." R. Simpson, in
C. M. Ingleby, ed., *Shakspere Allusion-Books* (1874), 1:xlviii, thought it
meant toleration in a religious or political sense. Machiavellianism and
Epicureanism were often linked; cf. *OED* Epicure 1.b: "one who rec-
ognizes no religious motives for conduct"; the 1589 quotation; 2C-C, 9.

[4] *wilfull . . . soule*] i.e., the punishment for apostasy is greater (deserves more) than that which I now experience (or fear I will, itself
extreme).

[5] *Defer not*] Cf. Dan. 9:19; *Nashe*, 2:120–21.

[6] *yong* Juvenall] i.e., almost certainly, Nashe. On this passage see
Appendix F. Cf. "tender juvenal" of *LLL*, I.ii.8, which, with the same
redundancy, may hint at the satirist, though *OED* cites no *juvenile* before
1625, and then only an adjective. Both places may play on Lat. *juvenilis*
or Fr. *juvénile* (see G. R. Hibbard's note to the Oxford Shakespeare).

[7] *lastly*] very lately, recently (*OED*, the first of two); but perhaps
"most recently," "last of all."

[8] *Comedie*] Surely stage-play, other senses not being encouraged by
the *OED*.

being blamed no man is injured.[1] Stop shallow water still running, it will rage,[2] or tread on a worme and it will turne: then blame not Schollers vexed with sharpe lines, if they reprove thy too much liberty[3] of reproofe.

And thou no lesse deserving than the other two, in some things rarer, in nothing inferiour; driven (as my selfe) to extreme shifts, a litle have I to say to thee:[4] and were it not an idolatrous oth,[5] I would sweare by sweet S. George,[6] thou art unworthy better hap, sith thou dependest on so meane a stay. Base minded men all three of you, if by my miserie you be not warnd[7]: for unto none of you (like mee) sought those burres to cleave: those Puppets (I meane) that spake from our mouths,

---

[1] *libertie . . . injured*] Cf. Jacques in *AYLI*, II.vii.47–49. Commonplace in discussions of satire and in disclaimers of satirists. *Liberty* (for freedom of expression) usually occurs in such contexts, probably from Horace, *Satires*, I.iv.5; see R. Burton, *Anatomy of Melancholy*, ed. H. Jackson (1964), 1:121–22, who quotes Horace and Martial. Cf. Harvey, the second letter, 1592 (*FL*, 15): "Oratours have challenged a speciall Liberty: and Poets claimed an absolute License; but no Liberty without boundes, nor any Licence without limitation. Invectives by favour have bene too bolde . . ."; and *Piers*, 140.

[2] *Stop . . . rage*] Cf. *NTL*, 8:84, 103; *FrF*, 8:205–6. For H. H. Holland, *Shakespeare, Oxford and Elizabethan Times* (1933), 212–13, this connects with Oxford, the "sharpe lines" being the preface to *Menaphon*, the "shallow water" and "worm" punning references to *Ox-ford* and *Ver*.

[3] *thy . . . liberty*] Cf. Tilley, L225: "Too much liberty spoils all."

[4] *And thou no lesse . . . .*] George Peele. Praised by Nashe in the preface to *Menaphon*, 1589, 3:323. He may have been considered gifted for inventiveness with pageants or plays or for verbal lyricism. The popular notion then and since has him in constant, near-desperate want.

[5] *idolatrous oth*] This oath is no more so than another—all are idolatrous.

[6] *by . . . George*] Mild asseveration. In sequent Qq, Cobb notes, *George* is in roman. The saint was perhaps suggested by Peele's patriotism: "an outrageous jingo in politics, a fire-eater and mouther of marvelous patriotic hyperboles" (C. F. T. Brooke, *Literary History of England*, ed. Baugh et al. [1948], 455). Peele's poem on the Order of the Garter, which makes much of St. George the patron, came out in 1593.

[7] *Base minded men. . . .*] On this famous passage, see Appendix G.

935 those Anticks[1] garnisht in our colours.[2] Is it not strange, that I, to whom they all have beene beholding: is it not like that you, to whome they all have beene beholding, shall (were yee in that case as I am now) bee both[3] at once of them forsaken? Yes trust them not: for there is an upstart Crow, beautified with our 940 feathers,[4] that with his *Tygers hart wrapt in a Players hyde*,[5] supposes he is as well able to bombast[6] out a blanke verse as

---

[1] *Anticks*] "Greene puts Shakespeare among the lowest and most scurrilous type of actors, the antic or mome; those grotesque characters with animal heads and bombast figures [who] came into Court revels with mops and mows, for dumb shows of detraction and scorn" (M. C. Bradbrook, *Shakespeare Survey* 15 [1962]: 64). The quotations in *OED* suggest that body paint was used.

[2] *garnisht in our colours*] i.e., pigments applied in make-up or costumes, metaphoric for "figures," "ornaments," "rhetorical modes." Cf. Nashe, *Anatomy*, 1589, 1:16: "[of those] who with Greene colours, seeke to garnish such Gorgonlike shapes."

[3] *both*] i.e., you three *and* I.

[4] *upstart . . . feathers*] Upstart (adj.), a buzz-word in the early 90s, occurs often before *pride*, *ambition*, and *greatness*. It refers not to Shakespeare's advent, but rather to his demeanor, his assumption of an undeserved status. *Beautified* occurs so often in Greene that it might have been identified with his style.

[5] Tygers . . . hyde] To Baldwin, Greene "usually substitutes the tiger for the wolf in the Biblical figure of the wolf in sheep's clothing, though twice in early work he has the original figure" (*Literary Genetics*, 50). Cf. *Mamillia*, 1580, 2:187–88: "Covering . . . the heart of the Tigre with the fleece of a Lambe." Warren B. Austin thinks Shakespeare filched his line from *FrF*, 1590—"[a courtesan] hides her clawes, but looks for her prey with the Tyger" (*Shakespeare Newsletter* 16 [Sept. 1966]: 30). The line parodied is *2H6*, I.iv.137 and on B2[v] *True Tragedy of Richard Duke of York*, (1595). *Players hyde* for *fleece of a lamb* may have been suggested by the name *Laneham* (Lat. *lana*, wool), an actor who headed one branch of the Queen's Men in 1592. W. Rankins' 1587 *Mirror of Monsters* may have suggested matter here: it attacks the players' hypocrisy and ingratitude (facs., 1973), Fi[r] (including): "More unnaturall are they then the Tygre," and "They will doo good to none of their benefactors." Cf. S. N[icholson]., *Acolastus His After-Wit*, 1600, line 265 (ed. 1876), 16: "O Woolvish heart, wrapt in a woman's hyde."

[6] *bombast*] Bombast was stuffing—"the material process by which unaccommodated man was endowed with bulbous curves" (G. D. Willcock, *Essays and Studies* 29 [1943]: 54); fig. for rhetorical elaboration.

the best of you[1]: and beeing an absolute *Johannes fac totum*,[2] is in his owne conceit the onely Shake-scene[3] in a countrey.[4] O that I might intreat your rare wits to be imploied in more profitable courses: and let those Apes imitate your past excellence, and never more acquaint them with your admired inventions.[5] I knowe the best husband of |F1ᵛ| you all will never prove an Usurer,[6] and the kindest of them all will never prove a kind nurse: yet whilest you may, seeke you better Maisters; for it is pittie men of such rare wits, should be subject to the pleasure of such rude groomes.[7]

945

950

---

[1] *best of you*] Generally taken to be Marlowe; see, e.g., C. F. T. Brooke, *Authorship of the Second and Third Parts of "King Henry VI"* (1912), 190.

[2] Johannes fac totum] "The fatal weakness of Johannes is rather his incompetence than his readiness to turn his hand to anything" (J. A. K. Thomson, *Shakespeare and the Classics* [1952], 162). See Appendix G.

[3] *Shake-scene*] "One of those jealous deformations of the great name to which the great name seems to lend itself" (A. Burgess, *Shakespeare* [1970], 109). To suggest the boisterous passion of blank-verse tragedy. In the First Folio, Jonson would call forth the "thund'ring" tragedians of old "to heare thy Buskin tread, / And shake a Stage." H. J. Oliver thinks *shake* may have meant *steal*, as in Australian slang, in *N&Q* 224 (1974): 115. S. Burckhardt, *Shakespearean Meanings* (1968), 80–83, takes "Shake thy speres" of *Edward I* (line 699, ed. Hook), thought by some, since F. G. Fleay, to allude to Shakespeare, to be a revision by which Peele consciously "softens the line Greene has so sharply drawn between poets and players."

[4] *in a countrey*] "in *the* country" (McKerrow, in, ed., *Nashe*, 4:192).

[5] *imitate . . . inventions*] i.e., "act the plays they have already obtained from you" and "write no more plays for them" (H. O. White, *Plagiarism and Imitation During the English Renaissance* [1935], 102); "Never . . . let the players see anything but your finished (and paid-for) products. Those they will imitate; let them. But beware of sitting down with them to plan a new play, for they will first steal your ideas and then . . . your credit" (S. Burckhardt, *Shakespearean Meanings* [1968], 57). The glance at *imitatio* and *inventio* suggests the superiority of academics.

[6] *best . . . Usurer*] i.e., most provident, frugal. In other words, "I know the best of *them* [Shakespeare] will prove [or, perhaps, has turned out to be] an usurer" (E. A. J. Honigmann, *Shakespeare's Impact* [1982], 6). "If the sentence conceals any allusion it is certainly to Lodge" [who wrote against usury] (P. Drew, *Studies in English Literature* 7 [1967]: 61).

[7] *groomes*] servants (contemptuous). The Queen's Men from 1583 on "were sworne the Queenes servants, and were allowed wages, and liveries as groomes of the chamber" (E. Howe in Stow's *Annals*, 1615, 697;

In this I might insert two more,[1] that both have writ against these buckram Gentlemen:[2] but lette their own workes serve to witnesse against their owne wickednesse, if they persevere to maintaine any more such peasants. For other new-commers, I leave them to the mercie of these painted monsters, who (I doubt not) will drive the best minded to despise them: for the rest,[3] it skils not though they make a jeast at them.[4]

But now returne I againe to you three, knowing my miserie is to you no newes: and let mee hartily intreat you to be warned by my harms. Delight not (as I have done) in irreligious oathes; for from the blasphemers house, a curse shall not depart.[5] Despise drunkennes, which wasteth the wit, and maketh men all equall unto beasts. Flie lust, as the deathsman of the soule, and defile not the Temple of the holy Ghost.[6] Abhorre those Epicures, whose loose life hath made religion lothsome to your eares: and when they sooth you with tearms of Maistership, remember *Robert Greene*, whome they have often so flattered, perishes now for want of comfort. Remember Gentlemen, your

---

1631, 698); see E. K. Chambers, *Eliz. Stage*, 2:104–5.

[1] *two more* . . . .] The two continue as dramatists; thus Munday (for *Second and Third Blast*, 1580) and Rankins (for *Mirror of Monsters*, 1587). F. G. Fleay (1886 and 1891) and E. I. Fripp (1938) suggested Kyd and Wilson; H. C. Hart (1909) suggested Lodge as one; A. Acheson (1920), Lodge and Royden, and then (1922) Chapman for one; A. Brooks (1937 and 1943), Kyd; E. B. Everitt (1954), Lodge and Lyly; T. W. Baldwin (1959), Lodge and Munday; M. C. Bradbrook (1962), Gosson and Munday.

[2] *buckram Gentlemen*] i.e., fake gentlemen, alluding to the material out of which stage monsters were created, a coarse type of cloth stiffened with paste. Harvey has "Buckrame Giants" (twice, 1592, *FL*, 54–55); Nashe "buckram giants" (1592, 1:242); *2Hen6*, IV.vii.23, "buckram lord!"

[3] *rest*] i.e., of those who write for actors.

[4] *jeast*. . . .] In the epistle to *Perimedes* (1588) Greene complains of being attacked on stage; in *NTL*, 8:129, some, who have been "too lavish against that facultie [acting], have for their satiricall invectives been well canvased." Martin Marprelate was so ridiculed; Harvey, 1593, 2:213, complains of those "hired, to make a Playe of you" and of "whole Theaters of Jestes." *K-HD*, 42, has harlots complain of players "making jeasts of us."

[5] *from* . . . *depart*] Blasphemers, in Matt. 12:31, Mark 3:29, and Luke 12:10, shall never be forgiven.

[6] *defile* . . . *Ghost*] i.e., the body. See 1 Cor. 6:19, 3:17.

lives are like so many lighted Tapers, that are with care deliv- 970
ered to all of you to maintaine: these with wind-puft wrath may
be extinguisht,[1] which drunkennes put out, which negligence[2] let
fall: for mans time is not of it selfe so short, but it is more
shortned by sinne.[3] The fire of my light is now at the last snuffe,
and for want of wherewith to su-|F2^r|staine it, there is no 975
substance lefte for life to feede on. Trust not then (I beseech
ye) to such weake staies: for they are as changeable[4] in minde,
as in many attyres. Wel, my hand is tyrde, and I am forst to
leave where I would begin: for a whole booke cannot containe
their wrongs, which I am forst to knit up in some fewe lines of 980
words.

Desirous that you should live,
though himselfe be dying:

Robert Greene.

Now to all men I bid farewel in like sort, with this conceited 985
Fable of that olde Comedian *Aesope*.[5]

An Ant and a Grashopper walking together on a Greene, the
one carelesly skipping, the other carefully prying what winters

---

[1] *like . . . extinguisht*] Cf. Job 21:17, Prov. 13:9, 24:20, Matt. 5:16.
Perhaps recalling parables of Wise and Foolish Virgins and of Talents
(both in Matt. 25). H. Crosse, *Virtue's Commonwealth*, 1603 (ed. 1878),
123–24, mixes phrases from here with his own comment.
[2] *negligence*] "Negligence [is] when we either altogether pretermit
[disregard], or more lightly passe over, the thing we ought seriously to
ponder" (Nashe, *Anatomy*, 1589, 1:42).
[3] *mans . . . sinne*] Cf. Ps. 89:47, 1 Cor. 7:29, Prov. 10:27.
[4] *changeable*] The *chameleon-comedian* comparison, common and
present here, occurs in *DC-C*, 37.
[5] *Comedian* Aesope] Probably "comic poet" (*OED* 2, with 1581
first), though possibly "comic actor." There was a long tradition of
presenting Aesop on stage. Perhaps used (with "*olde*") to distinguish the
fabulist from a tragic actor of this name sometimes alluded to, as by Nashe,
in *Pierce*, 1592, 1:215 (see McKerrow's note). Chettle describes Greene as
"the only Comedian of a vulgar writer in this country," in *K-HD*, 13. On
the treatment of this fable, see Appendix H. A reduced version in prose
is in H. Crosse, *Virtue's Commonwealth*, 1603 (ed. 1878), 131–32.

88

provision was scattered in the way: the Grashopper scorning (as
wantons will) this needlesse thrift (as hee tearmed it) reprooved
him thus:

> *The greedy miser thirsteth still for gaine,*
> *His thrift is theft, his weale works others woe:*
> *That foole is fond which will in caves remaine,*
> *When mongst faire sweets he may at pleasure goe.*

To this the Ant perceiving the Grashoppers meaning, quickly
replyde:

> *The thriftie husband spares what unthrift spends,*
> *His thrift no theft, for dangers to provide:*
> *Trust to thy selfe, small hope in want yeeld friends,[1]*
> *A cave is better than the deserts wide.* |F2ᵛ|

In short time these two parted, the one to his pleasure, the
other to his labour. Anon Harvest grew on, and reft from the
Grashopper his woonted moysture.[2] Then weakly skipt hee to
the medowes brinks: where till fell winter he abode. But storms
continually powring, hee went for succour to the Ant his olde
acquaintance, to whom hee had scarce discovered his estate,[3]
but the waspish little worme made this reply.

> *Packe hence (quoth he) thou idle lazie worme,*
> *My house doth harbor no unthriftie mates:*
> *Thou scorndst to toile, and now thou feelst the*
> *   storme,*
> *And starvst for food while I am fed with cates.*
> *Use no intreats, I will relentlesse rest,*
> *For toyling labour hates an idle guest.*

The Grashopper, foodlesse, helplesse and strengthles, got
into the next brooke, and in the yeelding sand digde for himselfe a pit: by which hee likewise ingrav'de this Epitaph.

> *When Springs greene prime arrayd me with delight,*

---

[1] *small . . . friends*] i.e., "friends offer little hope (to those) in want."

[2] *woonted moysture*] necessary bodily fluids.

[3] *scarce discovered . . .*] only just revealed, with a quibble: "his estate
to be scarce."

And every power with youthfull vigor fild,   1020
Gave strength to worke what ever fancie wild:
I never feard the force of winters spight.

When first I saw the sunne the day begin,
And dry the Mornings tears from hearbs and grasse;
I little thought his chearefull light would passe,   1025
Till ugly night with darknes enterd in.
    And then day lost I mournd, spring past I wayld,
    But neither teares for this or that availde. | F3ʳ |

Then too too late I praisd the Emmets paine,
That sought in spring a harbor gainst the heate: 1030
And in the harvest gathered winters meat,
Preventing famine, frosts, and stormy raine.

My wretched end may warn Greene[1] springing
    youth
To use delights, as toyes that will deceive,   1035
And scorne the world before the world them leave:
For all worlds trust, is ruine without ruth.
    Then blest are they that like the toyling Ant,
    Provide in time gainst winters wofull want.

With this the Grashopper yeelding to the wethers extremitie,   1040
died comfortles without remedy. Like him my selfe: like me,
shall all that trust to friends or times inconstancie. Now faint I
of my last infirmity,[2] beseeching them that shall burie my bodie,
to publish this last farewell written with my wretched hand.

Fœlicem fuisse infaustum.[3]   1045

---

[1] Greene] immature, fresh and lively (play on *Greene*). Everyone
knew Prov. 6:6–9: "Go to the Emmet, thou sluggarde, consider her
wayes, and learne to be wyse...."

[2] *Now faint...*] Cobb, among others, notes (cccii) a parallel with G.
Whetstone's *Rock of Regard*, 1576 (ed. Collier), 320: "I faint, I faint! my
life will needes away, / False Frenos now of force must yeeld to death."

[3] Fœlicem ... infaustum] See note to the title-page motto.

A letter written to his wife, founde
with this booke after his death.[1]

The remembrance of the many wrongs offred thee, and thy
unreproved vertues, adde greater sorrow to my miserable state,
than I can utter or thou conceive. Neither is it lessened by
consideration of thy absence, (though shame would hardly let
me behold thy face) but exceedingly aggravated, for that I
cannot (as I ought) to thy owne selfe reconcile my selfe, that
thou mightst witnes my inward woe at this instant, that have
made |F3ᵛ| thee a wofull wife for so long a time. But equall
heaven hath denide that confort, giving at my last neede like
succour as I have sought all my life:[2] being in this extremitie as
voide of helpe, as thou hast beene of hope. Reason would, that
after so long wast,[3] I should not send thee a child to bring thee
greater charge: but consider he is the fruit of thy wombe, in
whose face regarde not the Fathers faults so much, as thy owne
perfections. He is yet Greene, and may grow straight, if he be
carefully tended[4]: otherwise, apt enough (I feare mee) to follow
his Fathers folly. That I have offended thee highly I knowe,
that thou canst forget my injuries I hardly beleeve: yet perswade I my selfe, if thou saw my wretched estate, thou couldst
not but lament it: nay certainly I know thou wouldst. All my
wrongs muster themselves before mee, every evill at once
plagues mee. For my contempt of God, I am contemned of
men[5]: for my swearing and forswearing, no man will beleeve me:
for my gluttony, I suffer hunger: for my drunkennes, thirst: for

---

[1] A letter . . . death] On this letter, see Introduction, 10–11.

[2] *like . . . life*] i.e., none (he has never asked any). This may refer to
a reconciliation specifically: he does not now get that which he has not
sought before—heaven is consistent (*"equall"*). Something may be
omitted: *to give*, perhaps, following *sought*.

[3] *wast*] (a period of) wastefulness or prodigality. "So long wast"
suggests *wait* as the first thought or in MS. The spelling *wast* was common. It occurs at line 632.

[4] *grow . . . tended*] Cf. *Disput.*, 43: "Had they bent the wand while it
had beene greene, it woulde have been pliant," and 53.

[5] *of men*] by men.

my adultery, ulcerous sores. Thus God hath cast me downe,[1] that I might be humbled: and punished me for example of other sinners:[2] and although he strangely[3] suffers me in this world to perish without succor, yet trust I in the world to come to find mercie, by the merites of my Saviour to whom I commend thee, and commit my soule.

Thy repentant husband for his disloyaltie,

Robert Greene.

Fœlicem fuisse infaustum.[4]

FINIS. | F4ʳ |

---

[1] *God . . . downe*] Probably based on Jer. 6:15, 8:12 (Genevan).

[2] *example . . . sinners*] i.e., *to*; see *OED* (Example 3).

[3] *strangely*] in an unfriendly or unfavorable manner (*OED*). Omitted in later Qq.

[4] Fœlicem . . . infaustum] See note to the title-page motto.

Textual Notes

It would be very desirable to ascertain whether any alterations were made in [*Groatsworth*] after its first publication.
—Halliwell-Phillipps (1848)

page 41   This epistle is in roman.   5 pen,] Q2; —? Q1   7 worth, in] Q2; worth? In Q1   9 selfe:] Q2; —? Q1

page 42   This epistle is in italic.   20 sprigs] springs Q2   22 ye] you Q2   23 write] Q2; writ Q1   32 so] *om.* Q2

page 43   38 bounded] bound Q2–6   40 peace] space Q2–6   43 wealth] wealthy Q4–6   and] and of Q4; and of a Q5–6

page 44   49 tis] it is Q5–6   50 thers] there is Q6   53 many a yoong Gentleman] many gentlewomen Q2–3; many Gentlemen Q4–6   54 countries. Wise] this edition; —, wise Q1–2; —: wise Q3–6   boare] bare Q3–6

page 45   65 momentanie] momentarie Q2–3, 5–6   74 ye] you Q6   79 dayly] *om.* Q4   80 disease] diseases Q4   live] have lived Q4   82 intreated: witles,] Q4–6; —ₐ —: Q1–3   86 thou] you Q2–6

page 46   90 thinke] see Q2–6   92 gold!] Q2, 5–6; —? Q1; —, Q3; —ₐ Q4   94 creature!] Q2; —? Q1, 3, 5–6; —: Q4   96 liberality.] —? Q4   99 what not.] — —? Q2–6   105 pound] pounds Q4, 6   the] *om.* Q3–6   108 buy] buy him Q4   111 must I] I must Q4

page 47   120 Angry, . . . he),] this edition; Angryₐ . . . he)ₐ Qq   124 tell] telling Q2–6   126 returne] Q2–6; —, Q1 [B3ʳ]   130 sinn: loke] Q4; sinnloke: Q1–3; sinfull life: Q5; sinful life: looke Q6   134 Ah] As Q3; As for Q5–6   136 meanes] meanes possibly that Q3–6   142 excercises] —, Q2–6

page 48   149 is] *om.* Q3–6   153 forgeries,] Q2–6; —ₐ Q1   154 rais-inges] rasing Q2–6   158 tis] it is Q2–6   so] *om.* Q6   160 thy] Q2–6; the Q1   166 father,] Q2–6; — Q1   168 foole (sayd] Q1–5; —, — Q6

169 father)] Q2–5; —, Q1, 6 it not now] Grosart; it now Q1, 3–6; it. now Q2 174 the Name] that Name Q4

page 49 177 thy] Q2–6; thine Q1 183 so] *om.* Q2–6 185 it, laying] Q2–6; —ˌ — Q1 190 loud] aloud Q4

page 50 206 many] Q3–6; *om.* Q1–2 216 are] are so Q2–6 219 procure any] procure a man any Q2–6 220 obligation: in this Citie,] —ˌ — — —: Q4 221 and cause of solace,] any cause of solace? Q4 224 howsever] howsoever Q2–6 226 sundrye] certaine Q2–6

page 51 229 ye] you Q5–6 234 will] shall Q6 236 perticularities] particulars Q4 242 said,] Q4; —. Q1–3, 5; —; Q6 243 tis] it is Q2–6 245 all: well,] Q3–6; —, —ˌ Q1; —: —ˌ Q2 best, said *Roberto,*] Q2–6; —ˌ — —ˌ Q1 246 ye] you Q6 your] our Q2–6 248 toward] towards Q2–6

page 52 252 come] came Q2–6 256 a lute] her Lute Q6 259 *Fie*] —, Q3–6 260 *joy:*] —ˌ Q6 263 *first*] —, Q6 A B C] A B C. Q3–6 266 *led*] Q2–6; *lead* Q1 267 no,] —; Q5–6 268 *prove*] —, Q2–6 *so,*] —: Q2; —. Q3–6 269 *Fie*] —, Q3–6 270 *joy,*] —: Q4–6 271 *me,*] —ˌ Q3–4 274 *faine,*] —ˌ Q3 276 *disdaine.*] —, Q4

page 53 278 *prove*] —, Q2–6 *changings*] *changing* Q3–6 *so,*] —: Q2–6 279 *Fie*] —, Q5–6 280 *youthes*] *youth,* Q2 284 guile] Q4; guilt Q1–3, 5–6 285 her (1st)] the Q2–6 288 at lest] at the least Q6 289 father).] this edition; father) Qq world] wonder Q6 290 new] *om.* Q2–6 292 as if he ment] as though he went Q2–6 293 love] loves Q6

page 54 300 What,] this edition; —ˌ Qq springs] spring Q5–6 301 ye] you Q6 or . . . subject?] *om.* Q4 307 excellence] excellencie Q2–6 Brother, said *Lucanio,*] Q3–5; —ˌ — —ˌ Q1–2, 6 309 win] *om.* Q2–6 her:] Q4–5; —? Q1–3; —, Q6 314 for] and Q6 hell:] Q5; —. Q1–3, 6; —, Q4 315 *ditis.*] Q2–3, 6; —, Q1 —: Q4 321 his] your Q2–4

page 55 325 led] Q3–6; lead Q1–2 335 diligence] deliverance Q2–6 339 lackt] wanted Q6 341 performe] *om.* Q6 342 in] on Q6 343 amazeth] amazed Q2–6 345 were] was Q3–6 amated] amazed Q3–6

page 56 350 *Roberto,*] Q4; —ˌ Q1–3, 5–6 353 blindes] binds Q4 357 *Lucanio;*] Q4–5; —ˌ Q1; —, Q2–3, Q6 358 this] that Q2–3, 5–6 scornes] scornes for Q3–5 360 speake, Gentlewoman,] this edition; —ˌ —, Q5–6; —ˌ —ˌ Q1–4 *Lucanio?*] Q1 (catchword), 2–3, 5–6; —ˌ Q1; —: Q4 361 wind] minde Q4 366 poynted] pointed a Q2 368 true loves] truelovers Q2–6

page 57 380 content] contented Q2–6 381 him] himselfe Q2–6 386 with] and Q6 page 58 388 replied,] Q6; —ˌ Q1; —. Q2–3; —: Q4; —; Q5 394 infortunate] unfortunate Q6 395 Nay,] Q3, 5–6; —ˌ Q1–2, 4 396 woord: for that] Q4–5; —ˌ — — Q1; —, — — Q2–3; —ˌ — —: Q6; 397 own,] Q4; —ˌ Q1–2, 5–6 399 this speech] these speeches Q2–6 403 *labra*] Q3–6; *labe* Q1–2 405 ye] you Q3–6 your] Q2–6; our Q1 406 ye] you Q3–6

page 59 410 Badger enquired] —, enquiring Q2–6 414 unevitable] inevitable Q6 419 short, by] Q2–6; —ˌ — Q1 426 shepheardes] shepheard Q2–6 429 shepheards] shepheard Q2–6 431 dogs] dog Q2– 6 werried] wearied Q2–4; worried Q5–6 432 dogs] the dogges Q2–6

page 60 440 daughter] daughter to Q5–6 442 perfections] perfection Q2–6 447 strangers,] strangers that Q6 458 practise] practice and drift Q3–6 464 protestations] protestation Q6 affect] affects Q3–6

page 61 470 await] wait Q5–6 472 with] *om.* Q4 474 salve] save Q2– 6 476 how,] Q3–5; —ˌ Q1–2, 6 thus,] Q4; —ˌ Q1–3, 5–6 479 com- ming.] Q4–6; —, Q1–3 484 expects] expecting Q4 489 me] thee Q2–6 490 alighting] lighting Q2–6 493 you] we Q2–6 494 who] whom Q6

page 62 500 time] tune Q5 506 Gentlewoman, inwardly] this edition; —ˌ — Qq 507 his] *om.* Q5–6 508 according] *om.* Q3–6 512 and] all Q2–6 513 of] to Q5–6 515 with] which Q6 517 post] past Q3–6 fetch] fetcht Q3–6 518 the] an Q2–4

page 63 527 disturbing] disturbing us Q2–6 wheres] where is Q2–6 528 Wife,] Q4–6; —ˌ Q1–3 bed,] Q4; —ˌ Q1–3, 5–6 532 speake,] Q2–6; —ˌ Q1 533 in the bed] in bed Q6 539 arises] arrived Q3–6 544 adjudged] judged Q2–6 550 nothing,] Q4; —ˌ Q1–3, 5–6 554 thanke] thanks Q3–6 557 the] *om.* Q4

page 64 562 Thats] That is Q2–6 565 cards?] Q5–6; —. Q1–4 I,] Q4; —ˌ Q1–3, 5–6 so] if Q2–6 at (2nd)] *om.* Q3–6 566 That] Thats Q3–4 568 content,] —ˌ Q1; contented Q2–6 576 desiring him to] Q4, 6; desiring to Q1–3, 5 had determined] determined Q6

page 65 585 spake] speake Q3–5 586 theres] there is Q2–6 the] her Q2–6 593 No,] this edition; —ˌ Qq poore] more Q3–6 599 askest] asked Q2–6 600 forsaken] forsaking Q3–6 602 No, hypocrite,] this edition; —ˌ —, Qq

page 66 609 him] him of Q2–4 612 were] Q3–6; was Q1–2 619 *in*] *to* Q2–3, 5 620 *pride,*] —: Q4 622 *this*] —, Q2–5 *vices*] *vies* Q6 623 *wits*] —, Q5 *this*] *the* Q3–6 *converse,*] —ˌ Q3–4 624 *shoes,*] —ˌ Q3–6; *showes* Q4 625 *foes,*] —ˌ Q3 626 *the*] *their* Q2–3, 5–6 *disperse.*] —, Q6

page 67   629 *dangerous,*] —; Q5–6   632 *bring*] *brings* Q3–6   *hast*]
hastes Q3–6   634 earth] ground Q2–6   640 Gentleman, quoth hee,]
Q5–6; —ˏ — —ˏ Q1–4   641 you] your Q4   643 may] will Q2–6   645
you (1st)] your Q2–6   you (2nd)] your Q6

page 68   652 easily,] Q2, 4; —ˏ Q1, 3, 5–6   662 its] it is Q2–6   664
tis] it is Q2–6

page 69   671 *Roberto?*] —ˏ Q3–6   674 twas] it was Q2–6   675 to] of
Q2–6   680 its] it is Q2–6

page 70   683 thought] thought it Q3–6   in respect] to — Q2–6   of]
om. Q3–6   684 and] *om.* Q3–6   686 after] heereafter Q2–6   690 with]
withall Q2–5; with all Q6   697 his shooes] his hoes Q3, 5; and also
Q4; and Q6   699 unkindnes] kindness Q2–6

page 71   704 best] *om.* Q3–6   705 this] his Q2–6   709 did] did he Q2–
6   718 afore-hand] before hand Q5–6   720 slightly] sleightly Q2–6

page 72   725 they] they that Q6   726 his in] in his Q5; in Q6   beside]
besides Q3–6   729 casts] caste Q3–6

page 74   743 round as a] round a Q2   748 needes] *om.* Q3–6   753
gone,] Q2–6; —ˏ Q1   754 saw] Q5–6; see Q1–4   761 One] the one
Q5–6   762 the other] one other Q4   763 sodenly dyde] dyed suddenly
Q3–6

page 75   768 and by] by Q6   771 *Roberto* to bee] Q5–6; Roberto bee
Q1–4   774 lying] living Q2–6   782 parts] part Q3–6   784 now] new
Q2   788 *world,*] —ˏ Q3–6

page 76   791 *To length*] *To lengthen* Q2; *T'outlength* Q3–6   *forlorne.*] —
ˏ Q3; —, Q4–5   792 *borne,*] —. Q3, 5–6   793 *shun,*] —ˏ Q3   794
undone.] —ˏ Q6   795 *Love,*] —ˏ Q3–6   796 *advizde;*] —. Q3; —, Q4;
—ˏ Q6   798 *despizde.*] —ˏ Q3, 5; —: Q4, 6   800 *thought*] *thoughts* Q2–
6   *Love;*] —, Q2–5; *love was,* Q6   *delight;*] —, Q3–6   802 *want,*] —ˏ
Q2–6   *wit;*] —, Q2–6   803 *reft;*] —, Q3–6   804 *Wants . . . fit,*] (— . . .
—) Q6   *fit,*] Q4; —ˏ Q1; *sit*ˏ Q2; *sit,* Q3, 5; *sit*) Q6   805 *left:*] —, Q3,
5; —. Q4; —ˏ Q6   806 *heavens*] —, Q3–4   *gifts*] *gift* Q6   *bereft:*] —ˏ
Q3; —, Q4; —; Q5–6   810 *restorde:*] —, Q3, 5–6   811 *give?*] —, Q4;
—; Q6   812 *be deplorde?*] then deplore? Q2–3, 5   813 *abhorde.*] —, Q3–
4; —; Q5–6   814 *wonne,*] —ˏ Q3   815 *spent,*] —ˏ Q5–6   816 assaults!]
—? Q1–3, 5–6; —: Q4   820 yee] you Q2–6

page 77   825 any man was yet] yet was any man yet Q3; yet was any
man Q4–6   827 with mee together] together with me Q6   828 this]

om. Q3–6 834 First] *om.* Q6 836 to] unto Q5–6 837 moved] Q3–6; mocked Q1–2 839 and] *om.* Q2–6

page 78 841 abstain,] Q2–5; —ʌ Q1; —; Q6 847 doore] doores Q6

page 79 863 strive] straine Q4 864 vanish] vanish away Q2–6 866 example] examples Q2–6 872 obedient to] — at Q2–6 876 I] *om.* Q2–4

page 80 884 to beware . . . you] *om.* Q4 893 felt] left Q2–6 896 peevish] punish Q2–6

page 81 904 brocher] brother Q2–6 907 *iudicia!*] Q3–6; —? Q1–2

page 82 911 but to] unto Q2–6 920 wordes:] —? Q5–6

page 83 924 or] *om.* Q2–6 925 Schollers] Schollers who are Q3–6 sharpe] sharpe and bitter Q3–6 932 you be] ye be Q2–6 934 spake] speake Q2–6

page 84 938 as] that Q2–6 at once of them] of them at once Q3–6 940 *hart*] *head* Q4

page 85 943 Shake-scene] Shake-sence Q6 945 those] these Q3–6 948 never] not Q6 950 pleasure] pleasures Q2–6

page 86 953 workes] worke Q3–6 963 maketh] making Q2–4

page 87 970 lighted] light Q3–6 972 which . . . which] with . . . with Q5–6 973 is not of it selfe] of it selfe is not Q2–6 975 for] the Q2–Q6 976 lefte] *om.* Q3–6 977 ye)] you) Q6 to] left to Q3–5 980 their] the Q5–6 985 like] this Q2–6 986 that] the Q2–6

page 88 992 *miser*] —, Q4 993 *woe:*] —, Q3; —; Q5–6 998 *unthrift*] unthrifts Q2–6 *spends,*] —ʌ Q3; —; Q4 999 *thrift*] *thrift's* Q4 *provide:*] —, Q3, 5–6; —; Q4 1000 *friends,*] —ʌ Q3; —: Q4 1001 *wide*] *wilde* Q3–6 1004 skipt] skips Q2–6 1008 waspish] *om.* Q2–6 1009 (*quoth he*)] , —— , Q4;(— *she*) Q5–6 1012 *storme,*] —ʌ Q3, 5–6 1013 *food*] —, Q3–6 *cates.*] —, Q3, 5–6; —: Q4 1016 Grashopper, foodlesse] this edition; —ʌ — Qq 1017 for] *om.* Q2–6 1018 hee likewise] likewise he Q2–4

page 89 1021 *wild:*] —, Q3–6 1023 *sunne*] —, Q6 1024 *grasse;*] —, Q3–6 1026 *in.*] —, Q3–6 1027 *lost*] —, Q4 *past*] —, Q4 1030 *heate:*] —, Q3–6 1031 *harvest*] —, Q4 1032 *Preventing*] *Perceiving* Q2–6 1033 *warn*] —, Q4 *youth*] —, Q3–6 1036 *world* (1st)] —, Q3–6 *leave:*] —, Q3–6 1037 *worlds*] *the worlds* Q6 1038 *Ant,*] —. Q3 1039 *winters wofull*] *wofull winters* Q3–6 1040 extremitie] extremit Q1–2

page 90 1048 the many] many Q2–6 1051 hardly let me] let me
hardly Q2–6 1059 wast] waste Q2–6 1061 faults] *om.* Q3–6 1068
before] about Q2–6 1074 other sinners] others sinne Q2–6 al-
though] though Q6 strangely] *om.* Q2–6

page 91 1080 *Fœlicem....*] *om.* Q4 1081 *Finis*] *om.* Q3–6

Appendix A

The Contributions of "I. H." to the Later Quartos

Beginning with the 1617 quarto, this dedication replaces the original two and the poem "Greenes Epitaph" is added at the end. Both are signed "I. H.," presumably John Hind or Hynd (attributed to him in the Huth Catalogue, 1880, 2:624). Walter R. Davis discusses the plagiarisms from Greene in Hind works of 1604 and 1607 (*Notes and Queries* 214 [1969]: 90–92). The BM Catalogue (1946, 24:88) suggests Jasper Heywood.

To Wittie Poets, or Poeticall Wittes

A *Witte*, that runnes this sublunarie *Maze*, and takes but *Nature* for its *Originall*, makes *Reason*, and *Judgement*, a payre of false spectacles, where-through to take an imperfect survey of things *above earth*; and so leaping over the *Light* of *divine direction*, falles hudwinckt into the pitfall of its owne Folly: For a *Wit* unsanctified, is the Divels *Anvile*, whereon he forges the engines of *selfe-ruine*. This is the reason, that so many *witworn Ideots*, after they have descended from the high stand of *Contemplation*, to looke into themselves, are forced (the day after the Fayre) to howle out this olde B*allad* made in Hell:

> *Ingenio perii, qui miser ipse meo:*
> *Wit, whither wilt thou? woe is me;*
> *Th'hast brought me to this miserie.*

Under the wings of a *wit naturall*, are hatcht these three *unluckie-Birdes: Impudence, Selfe-conceit, Emulation*. *Impudence* turnes the Key of *Contempt*, and lets in *hard Opinion* to passe in *Judgement* against the *Generall*, still bearing out her owne *Disease* with a stolne face: her *forme* is reflected from the glasse of *Flatterie*, wherein shee showes fayre, others foule; and doting on *Figures* falsely presented, scornefully kickes downe perfect *Knowledge* to the lowest Region of Disgrace.

Selfe-conceit, shee prodigiously studies to put out the *Light of wit*, by seeming to know beyond the reach of *Reason*, as if shee had miraculously discovered some stand from off the earth, above the sight of *Humanitie*, from whence over-looking all, makes it her owne *glorie*, hypercritically to reprove others.

Emulation, she was nurc't by a shee-Toad; shee never lins swelling, till shee burst her selfe, and poysons others: Shee speakes none faire, but a Barber; and him, for feare too; lest he should show her the tricke of a Cut-throat: She will be *none*, where shee may not be *best*: Shee's ever strugling to clamber up to the narrow toppe of absolute *perfection*, and there to sit alone, whilst the desertfull *Hopes* of true *Discretion*, willingly give up their *Care*, and silently content to stay *below*, or come *behind*. These prenominated, are the three bold Bayards, that justle and shoulder for a sitting place in this Worlds wide *Court of Requests*, when *Vertue* and *Knoweldge*, know it better manners to stand and wait.

The bestiall gutlings of this fulsom-feeding age, fall upon a piece of piping-hot *Poetrie*, as on a *Christmas Pie*, they dabble their durtie fingers in't; stuffe up their stomackes; belch out a soure *Censure*, and then regardlesly thrust it to the lower end o'th table: so that, notwithstanding she come cladde in the richest habite of *Skill*, and pranked out in the liveliest colours of *Conceit*; yet before *Censures* blinkling eye, she appeares but an ill-favoured Dowdie.

Poetrie affoords better measure of *Charitie*, then *Poperie*: For, to lend the world a furnish of *Witte*, shee layes her *owne* to pawne: And for her *Humilitie*, that's over-running full: for shee will kisse the shadow of a gowtie-toes shadow, and he crowching at the foote of an *Epistle*, to watch the fall of some *Great mans* gracefull *looke*; and at last, for her labour, perhaps, be popt i'th mouth with a *Churles Almes*, that's *Nothing*. *Poetrie* and *Beggerie* are *twin-born-brats*: they have one *fate* from *Birth*, one *fall* to *Death*; and both *unfortunate*.

Of all other *creatures*, your *Poet* lives most in, and most out of danger; and that in two respects: He lives most in danger, to perish for want of *Competencie*; and contrariwise, he lives most out of danger, for ever being rifled; because hee never caries anything about him, worth playing the theefe for: To be a *Poet*, and have *meanes to bee so*, is not *to be* at all: for hee must put off *himselfe*, and compose his Parts after the *vulgar forme*; be *new*, with mens *new affections*: he must not run a counter-course, out from the scent of those *Humours*, the present times approve: Above all, hee must deifie *Pride*; shee must have tapers of *supple soothings*, set up before her illustrious *outside*; no matter, if the *Soule* within, sitte poorely without *Light*. The true *Degree*, and just *Height* of her swolne *Sublimitie*, must not bee taken, right *as it is*, but as it *seemes to be*: after this, *Imagination* steps out, and (as *Isis* Asse was) guls her with this beleefe; That those *Honours* are bestowed on her, when indeed they are otherwise offered up to the *painted Idoll* she carries.

O Spirit of Distraction! That sacred *Learning*, the happie *Birth* of Heaven; who ha's *Reward* and *Riches* dwelling within her selfe; should be forc't by the furious Tyrant *Want*, so to prostrate her unblemisht *Bodie*, as to committ folly with *Earth*, and besoyle her State of *Cleerenesse*, for so grosse a benefit as Breath?

Wit, may not unaptly be termed, the worlds *goggle-eyde Lampe*; which illightning all, darkens its owne: and to feed others, devoures it selfe: *Wit* and *Honesty* cannot abide each others Company; for *Necessitie* is the *go-betweene*, to set 'em at oddes. *Wit* is a skilfull Midwife; it can deliver its *owner* of a bigge-bellied Purse, and bring the same man to bed of a foule shirt. There's an English Proverbe, that, *Wit runs a wooll-gathering*: and good reason too: for its commonly *thrid-bare*. A *Poet* and his *Wit*, must be like *Adams* and his *Ape*; they must trudge together from place to place, to shew trickes for a living; and that too, (like a Witches) ever bare and base: Is not that *Wit* superlatively sottish? which disburses large summes of *Labour*, and takes upon trust, inestimable treasures of *Time*, for Doomes-day repayment, onely to purchase a *puffe of praise*; and yet at last, leaves to his Heyre nothing, but the Fee-simple of *Povertie*? That *Life* therefore is but *Death* above-ground, which propounds *Griefe* its *Gaine*; and affliction its end and period.

But here I meete with an *Exit*: the *Prologue's* ended, and I must off: Now *Reader*, (for I will not call thee, *gentle*, till I know whether thou wilt bite or no) behold a drie and *withered shadow*, (which once was *Greene*) appeare in his native colour; new dipt, and a fresh glosse set on him; ready to enter upon the Stage of triall, to answere upon's Cu, and speake his owne part.

Yours; if not, the care's taken,

I. H.

GREENES EPITAPH

Discoursed Dialogue-wise betweene Life *and* Death.

LIFE.

Stay grizly *Thanatos*, pull backe thy spleene,
Triumpher over Tombes, what hast thou done?
To blast the Muses *Lawrell*, which was *Greene*;
Minerva's nurse child, great *Apollo's* sonne:
O what i'st, made of Mold, thy stabbe can shun?
    Sure th' hast no eyes to dart at randon so;
    To strike the *Cedar*, let the Mush-rumpe grow.

Where *Life* is lov'd, tha'rt too too quicke to kill,
And to epitomize, with pangs, their joy:
Where *Life* is loath'd, tha'rt slow, and backward still,
And dost adjourne their *death* with *lifes annoy*:
Thus Tyrant-like, the *Best*, dost still *destroy*:
    To some thou art a sterne unbidden guest,
    But who implore thy helpe, thou helpest least.

DEATH.

Why wouldst creepe longer on this *dustie Round*,
Where *wealth's* but *want*; where Treasures *won*, but lost;
Where all good *Hopes*, in one *ill-hap*, are drown'd,
In some things, all: in all things, some are crost;
And they but *little*, that possesse the *most*.
    Unmixed Joyes, to none on earth befall,
    Who least ha's *some*, who most, ha's never *all*.

For that, must I his *purer Part* unshroude,
(A Kings commaund cannot withstand my right)
And give his prison'd *Soule*, midst mistie Cloud,
A larger Horizon t'emblaze *her light*:
Her *Beauty* then appearing Sun-like bright,
    Shall shunne the earth, to shine (fore *Angels eyes*)
    In *Blisse*, above the Star-bespangled skies.

LIFE.

You sacred Sisters, from whose Bosome's cropt,
A fresher *Flowers* then by *Alcinous* bred:
Through your Eyes Lymbecke, let your loves be dropt,
(Though often true that more oft ha's been sayd,
The fayrer *Flower*, the sooner withered)
    To keepe him *Greene*, with world out-wearing Rimes,
    To th'admiration of succeeding Times.

Hee, whose gold-typped, Eare-attracting *Toung*,
With rare *Cyllenian* Musicke charmed so,
As Marbles danc'd, when *Thebes Musitian* sung.
Let rowling Teares in Pleni-tides oreflow,
For losse of *Englands* second *Cicero*.
    To make's *not being*, be, as *he* hath beene,
    Greene, never-wither'd, ever-wither'd *Greene*.

                  I. H.

Appendix B

The Results of Warren B. Austin's Computer Study

Part of the "Summary" of *A Computer-Aided Technique for Stylistic Discrimination: The Authorship of "Greene's Groatsworth of Wit."* U.S. Dept. of Health, Education, and Welfare. Office of Education. Project No. 7–G-036. Grant No. OEG–1–7–070036–4593. (Washington, D.C., 1969), ix–xi.

When the contrasting rates of usage of these ten classes of language variables [just listed, now presented in some detail] were applied as authorship tests to the *Groatsworth of Wit*, the frequency patterns found in the questioned work differed in every case from those that had been established as characteristic of Greene; and in every case they matched those established as typical of Chettle. For the words in which their usages contrasted most markedly, the 29 Greene-favored words occur collectively in the *Groatsworth of Wit* at less than one-fourth their average collective frequency in Greene's prose, whereas the 21 Chettle-favored words occur in the *Groatsworth* at almost precisely the rate to be expected if the book was another sample of Chettle's prose.... Of the seventeen high-frequency words which qualified as discriminators, fourteen have frequency-distribution patterns in the *Groatsworth* that are unlike Greene's and similar to Chettle's; all five such words showing the greatest Differential Ratios between the two writers (*a, and, as, by,* and *so*) have patterns more like Chettle's than Greene's. Of 33 relatively uncommon words and word-senses sifted out of the *Groatsworth* by pre-established criteria, none appears in the Greene corpus, whereas five appear in the much smaller Chettle corpus.

For the group of prefix discriminators, the frequency rate of words beginning with these prefixes in the *Groatsworth* (29.3) differs decidedly from Greene's average rate (18.8) and agrees well with Chettle's (31.3).* [*All frequencies are given as average number of occurrences per 1000 words.] And for the suffix discriminators as a group the

Groatsworth rate of 17.1, almost double Greene's typical rate of 9.1, matches the Chettle rate of 17.6.... The *Groatsworth* also exhibits Chettle's practice in using reflexive pronouns and plural forms of the gerund at a markedly higher rate than Greene.

For all ten categories of compound words in which the two writers have distinctively different rates of usage (Greene's being in each case lower than Chettle's), the frequencies in the *Groatsworth* reflect Chettle's practice, not Greene's. ... In the use of parentheses (excluding conventional usages), the *Groatsworth* rate of 4.81 is five and one-half times Greene's average rate of .86 and almost four times the highest rate (1.34) found in the five Greene works concorded, whereas it is consistent with Chettle's average rate of 3.69 and virtually identical with his highest rate (4.69) in a single work.

Study of the word-order positions of prepositional phrases revealed that, in every one of the twelve discriminating categories, the *Groatsworth of Wit* had rates of inversion from three to twenty-five or more times higher than Greene's and remarkably similar to Chettle's. ...

When the *Groatsworth* was checked for a number of idiosyncratic usages of the two writers, Chettle's authorship was strikingly confirmed. Greene *invariably* uses the combinative forms *howsoever, whatsoever, whensoever, wheresoever,* and *whosoever,* avoiding the parallel *-ever* forms (*however, whatever,* etc.); but the *-ever* forms predominate in the *Groatsworth,* as they do also in Chettle. Greene has the colloquial form *ye* only one-half of one percent of the times he uses the second person pronoun; the rate is 38% in Chettle and 19% in *Groatsworth.* Not only Chettle's distinctively higher frequencies for the prefix *un-* and the suffix *-less,* but also his unorthodox formations with these negative affixes are reflected in the *Groatsworth.* Greene has no case of the noun + present participle type of compound, which occurs at a rate of one per 5000 words in Chettle; three cases (*home-breeding, sun-darkening* and *wine-washing*) appear in the *Groatsworth.* Finally, four categories of prepositional phrase inversion that do not occur at all in the Greene corpus occur 36 times in Chettle and five times in the *Groatsworth.*

Appendix C

"Lamilias Fable"

Both Chettle and Nashe were quick to deny any part in *Groatsworth*, Chettle in the preface to *Kind-Heart's Dream* (ent. 8 December) and Nashe in the epistle to the second edition of *Pierce* (composed within a month of the entry of *Groatsworth*), calling it "a scald trivial lying pamphlet." McKerrow found it "difficult to understand the very strong terms in which [Nashe] alludes to [*Groatsworth*] unless indeed it contains references which we cannot now recognize."[1] The advice to Marlowe and the outburst against Shakespeare would have disturbed some, of course. What McKerrow apparently suspected but overlooked is an attack against Lord Burghley in a beast fable. The risk involved in printing this fable may account for the warning and possible attribution of responsibility carried in the allowance "uppon the perill of *Henrye Chettle*," by which peculiar entry Wright, the publisher, protected himself. The courtesan Lamilia gives the fable (lines 407ff.), after she and Roberto have conspired to fleece his rich but naive brother, in order to warn Roberto against a double cross.

Two features of this fable seem certain. First, after the public reaction to Spenser's *Mother Hubberd's Tale* in the *Complaints* volume (ent. 29 December 1590), any such fable would be taken to allude to serious matters involving those in high places. For some time now, based on indirect evidence, scholars have suspected that Spenser's volume was called in because of its fable of the fox and the ape. Now, with the recent discovery by Richard Peterson of a contemporary letter dated 19 March 1591, we can be absolutely sure.[2] Writing within two or three months of the publication of *Mother Hubberd's*,

---

[1] *Dreame*, ed. Harrison, 6–7; *Pierce*, ed. McKerrow, 1:154, with McKerrow's comment at 4:88 and on dating, 78–79. Where fuller references are required in the notes to the appendices, consult the Abbreviations section of the Introduction.

[2] For the text of the letter see Richard S. Peterson, "Laurel Crown and Ape's Tail," *Spenser Studies* (forthcoming). The best treatment of the allegorical significance of Spenser's fable is by Brice Harris, in *Huntington Library Quarterly* 4 (1940): 191–203.

the author describes how scandalous its fable was thought to be and notes the scarcity and high cost of the forbidden book. After *Mother Hubberd's*, an animal fable would put a book in great demand. Nashe's *Pierce* (ent. 8 August 1592) had an elaborate beast fable and beasts scattered throughout, to which Gabriel Harvey, who wanted Nashe to get into trouble for *Pierce*, alerted the authorities in *Four Letters*: "they can tell parlous Tales of Beares and Foxes, as shrewdlye as Mother Hubbard, for her life," and in *Pierce's Supererogation*: "my leisure will scarsely serve, to moralize Fables of Beares, Apes, and Foxes: (for some men can give a shrewd gesse at a courtly allegory)."[3] Nashe had repeatedly to defend himself: his only intention in presenting a fox, he said, was "to figure an hypocrite."[4] *"Lamilias Fable"* is designed to exploit the demand started by *Mother Hubberd's*, and it would have been read for the same kind of meaning. Greene, the apparent author, was beyond consequence.

Second, the fox in the fable would be taken for Burghley. The fox had long been a generalized emblem of malicious hypocrisy, as Nashe suggests. More recently, in allegories on the difficulties of the religious settlement, it represented Anglican churchman with covert Catholic sympathies.[5] But a fox in the early nineties has to be Burghley *because* of *Mother Hubberd's*. Nashe has Burghley in mind for the *Pierce* foxes, as Anthony G. Petti has shown, and Burghley conforms neatly to the role of the fox in our fable.[6] He was the chief marriage maker of his day, being, in Joel Hurstfield's view, which is based on Burghley's correspondence, "a matchmaker for all England."[7] He took special interest in and considerable profit from the marriages of his own wards, which included the choicest available during his tenure as Master of the Court of Wards. The badger here, having lost all family and friends, has become, in effect, a ward and is urged to marry by the fox. "It was imagined," Burghley's domestic biographer

---

[3] Ed. Harrison, 54–55; *Works of Harvey*, ed. Grosart, 2:54.

[4] *Strange Newes*, ed. McKerrow, 1:321.

[5] For the distinction between fox and wolf, the former being a sympathizer, the latter a professed Catholic, see F. M. Padelford in *Modern Philology* 11 (1913): 20. The only interpretation other than my own is M. C. Bradbrook's single remark that "the red-haired fox [is] also the red-haired Greene," in *Shakespeare Survey* 15 (1962): 67.

[6] See Petti's arguments in *Neophilologus* 44 (1960): 208–15; 45 (1961): 139–50; and *Essays and Studies* 16 (1963): 68–90.

[7] *The Queen's Wards: Wardship and Marriage under Elizabeth I.* 2d edn. (London: Frank Cass, 1973), 147.

tells us, that "he made infinite gain by the wards."[8] The gray, which
is either another, related fox or another badger (*gray* is regularly listed
in dictionaries of the time for *badger*), might stand for Gray's Inn,
Burghley's Inn, where he saw to it that his wards enrolled. While he
seems to have been busy at this time about arrangements for the marriage of one of his wards, Henry Wriothesley, Earl of Southampton,
of Gray's Inn, *Badger* does not clearly point to the earl or any of his
other wards. The fable relies, it seems, on this particular sphere of
activity for which Burghley was well known and criticized in order, by
association, to draw attention to activity in another sphere for which
he was not known and deserved criticism.

Two separate readings merit consideration and perhaps can be
made to accommodate each other. The fox-sheep-shepherd-dog motif
suggests controversies surrounding the effort by authorities to bring
about religious conformity. In this fairly common context, shepherds
are bishops, in particular those responsible for seeking out and con-
trolling nonconformists, which means Whitgift and Aylmer at work
through the Court of High Commission. The dogs are the pursui-
vants, justices, sheriffs, and spies in their service—"Lambethetical
whelps," as Martin Marprelate called them.[9] One word seems to
identify a name: the whelp is "yoonge" to suggest Richard *Young*,
Justice of the Peace for Middlesex, Whitgift's convenient tool. "No
man," according to Albert Peel, "was more active than Young in the
prosecution of religious dissidents, Catholic and Protestant, and there
are many illustrations of the odium he drew upon himself."[10] The
"wanton ewe stragling from the fold" must be the Church, with its
vast holdings—she "is lady of al these lawnds." "Her brother[,]
cheefe belweather of sundry flockes," is Christ, the lamb—"a Lambe
stode on mount Sion, and with him an hundreth, fortie and foure
thousand" (Rev. 14:1, Genevan). The Church, both sister and bride
of Christ (Cant. 5:2; Rev. 19), has wandered and, through the agency
of the fox, has given herself unto another.

Badgers are noncomformists, not recusants, and probably not even
Puritans in general but rather those farther to the left, that is, the
Separatists, called Brownists (after Robert Browne) and also, especial-
ly toward the end of the eighties and in the early nineties, called

---

[8] *Desiderata Curiosa Hibernica*, ed. Francis Peck (1723), 1:27, in Hurstfield,
Queen's Wards, 263.

[9] *The Protestation of Martin Marprelate*, in *The Marprelate Tracts: 1588, 1589*,
ed. William Pierce (London: James Clarke, 1911), 406.

[10] On Young's activities see Peel's account in, ed., *The Notebooks of John
Penry, 1593* (London: Royal Historical Society, 1944), xx, 49.

Barrowists (after Henry Barrow), who urged a complete break with the established Church. In his 1593 *Survey of the Pretended Holy Discipline*, Richard Bancroft complained of the growth, danger, and secrecy of "these newe upstartes [who] beginne to erecte in diverse places, theyr Barrowish Synagogues."[11] They were viewed with great perturbation by the officials, and Whitgift was determined to suppress them. Their leaders, John Greenwood and Henry Barrow, had been in jail, along with many of the faithful, since November 1587 and would be hanged in April 1593.

The *badger* may have been chosen because *Barrow* was close in sound and meaning to *burrow*, the hole the badger lived in: compare "Borow for Greys or Foxes" (*OED* Grey *sb.* 6, 1538). Bancroft plays on the two words in the 1593 quotation above. The term falls neatly alongside the other animal terms—wolf-fox-badger—along a spectrum of religious attitudes from right to left. The *OED* actually lists *badger* as one meaning of *barrow*, but does so with little confidence; in its one reference ("1552 *Huloet* Badger, barrow, brocke, or greye beaste.") it questions whether *barrow* is a misprint for *bausom* (still another word for *badger*). Barrow, we know, had been a member of Gray's Inn, was distantly related to Burghley ("partly for kindered"; through Burghley's marriage to Mildred Cooke), and was sequestered in Fleet prison (a true ward of state!), thus removed from family and friends.

The passage treats Separatists with less hostility than one might expect, representing itself, as it does, as being by Greene. He was of the party of the prelates, may have been in their pay as part of the counterattack against Martin, and had Sir Christopher Hatton as a patron. Nashe, his copesmate, had nothing kind to say about Brownists and Barrowists.[12] Greene's attitude, however, may have been recognized as mixed. He was from Norwich, "the centre of the Separatist movement" (William Pierce[13]), home of Robert Harrison, and place of Browne's first church. Barrow was from nearby Shipdam, and had attended Clare Hall, one of Greene's colleges (several years before Greene's residence). If we can believe the account given in *The Repentance of Robert Greene*, he was converted by a preacher at St. Andrews Church, Norwich, and after, before falling to his old ways, was ridiculed by his mates as a "Puritane and Presizian."[14] He appears to have attacked the Puritans only once, in a brief para-

---

[11] STC 1352, 428.
[12] See in particular *Pierce*, ed. McKerrow, 1:171–72.
[13] Ed., *Marprelate Tracts*, 187n.
[14] Ed. Harrison, 24.

graph in *A Quip*, and this he removed after the first edition.[15] The function of the fable by this reading, in any case, is to charge Burghley with abusing the Church and, incidentally, with an apparent if hypocritical support of the Separatists. The fable may rely on growing sympathy in London to the plight of the imprisoned Separatists and increased hostility to Whitgift.

It suggests that the real threat to the Church is Burghley, not the Separatists, in order to deflect hostility from Whitgift and restrict Burghley's influence with the commission on the Separatist issue (by publicly linking him to them). The Separatists themselves assumed that Burghley was sympathetic, and scholars attribute whatever relief they got to his influence, one that may have been diminishing in 1591–92. Whitgift had the queen's support. The pathetic record of Barrow's attempt to tap Burghley's power survives in unavailing letters and petitions. A major threat to the prelates was the ultimate loss of their source of wealth and power, the fear of which they typically transferred into a charge against the Puritans. To Nashe, who is the voice of Whitgift, Martinists and such like are "purchasers" and "brokers" intent on robbing the Church.[16] The fable makes a clear target of Burghley, much of whose vast estate was or was thought to be, in the words of his friend Camden, "wrung by way of inequitable exchange from the Church."[17]

A second reading refers to the troubles of Sir John Perrot, former Lord Deputy of Ireland and reputed to be the queen's half brother, by Henry. After a long and arduous investigation (which began in late 1589), Perrot was tried and convicted of treason in the spring of 1592. It was assumed then, and is now, that Perrot was brought down by enemies in Ireland, chiefly Adam Loftus, Archbishop of Dublin, largely through perjury, and by his old antagonist at court, Hatton. (The gossip that Perrot seduced the illegitimate daughter of

---

[15] E. H. Miller, in *Huntington Library Quarterly* 15 (1952): 279, gives the complete statement (the last clause of which was removed after the first edition): ". . . the world was never in quiet, [?] devotion, neighbourhood nor hospitalitie never flourished in this land since such upstart boies and shittle witted fooles becam of the ministrie, such, I means as *Greenwood Martin, Barrow, Wigginton,* and such rakehels."

[16] See, as examples, ed. McKerrow, 1:73, 94–95, 99, and 109.

[17] From *Annals*, 336, in A. B. Grosart, ed., *The Complete Works of . . . Edmund Spenser* (London), 1:87. Archbishop Parker on his deathbed is said to have charged Burghley with procuring the spoil of the Church (Strype, *Parker*, 2:431, in James Jackson Higginson, *Spenser's "Shepherd's Calendar" in Relation to Contemporary Affairs* [New York: Columbia Univ. Press, 1912], 123). For a fuller version of the case for Barrow in the fable, though my views have changed somewhat since, see *Studies in Philology* 84 (1987): 471–82.

Hatton, whom Elizabeth called her "sheep" or "mutton," does not seem relevant.) One long-standing criticism of Perrot, about which much was made at the time, stemmed from a proposal he had brought with him to Ireland: he had wanted to convert the income of St. Patrick's Cathedral into an endowment for a university. Though successfully resisted by Loftus and others, he never gave up this idea completely. Perrot's response to the criticism, to quote Richard Bagwell, was that "the idea had not been originated by him," which is true, and "that his instructions from the Privy Council, signed by Burghley himself along with others, would have warranted him in proceeding far more roughly than he had done."[18] While historians disagree on Burghley's attitude toward Perrot, it is possible that he sympathized with and supported Perrot insofar as he could.[19] Perrot was in Burghley's custody in February 1591. This reading places the responsibility for Perrot's troubles on Burghley, perhaps displacing it from Hatton (who had died in December 1591), and thus may be an argument for Greene's authorship. Burghley drew up a list of the charges against Perrot in November 1591, the trial took place in April 1592, and Perrot died in the Tower in September. In the summer of 1592 the business of the Privy Council, according to the *Acts*, was seriously obstructed because of "the multitude of Iryshe suitors that do repaire hether."[20] Perrot's status would have been of widespread interest.

The equation of *badger* with *Perrot* depends on the *gray* of the opening being taken as Lord *Gray* of Wilton, whom, as everyone knew, Perrot immediately *succeeded* as Lord Deputy. Instead of finding the *gray*, the Fox finds the *badger*. The badger was an appropriate symbol for Perrot because he was thoroughly identified with Pem*broke*shire (*brock* is the Celtic name for badger), his residence, estate, and career (before Ireland) being there, and because like the badger he was known to be pugnacious by temperament and tena-

---

[18] *Ireland Under the Tudors* (London), 3:134. For accounts of the trial see Pauline Henley, "The Treason of Sir John Perrot," *Studies* (Dublin) 21 (1932): 404–32; David Mathew, *The Celtic Peoples and Renaissance Europe* (London: Sheed and Ward, 1933), 225–29; Richard Berleth, *The Twilight Lords: An Irish Chronicle* (New York: Alfred A. Knopf, 1978), 239–42. In *Shakespeare's Lost Years in London: 1586–1592* (London: B. Quaritch, 1920), 131–49, Arthur Acheson argues that the Bastard in *Troublesome Raigne of King John* is Perrot.

[19] Cf., e.g., Bagwell, 3:228, and Mathew, 222.

[20] On 24 June and, later, on 28 July, there were complaints and consequently restrictions set against access to the court; see *Acts of the Privy Council, 1591–1592*, 587, and ibid., *1592*, 82f. See also the account in Thomas M. Cranfill and Dorothy Hart Bruce, *Barnaby Rich* (Austin: Univ. of Texas Press, 1953), 68–69.

cious when engaged. "*Hattons* sly smoothness undermined [Perrot's] open roughness," according to David Lodge.[21] There may also be some play on the name *Perrot*—one thinks of a French pronunciation for *Perrault* that would resemble *barrow*.

Neither of these readings offers much help in dating this section, Barrow's confinement covering a period from late 1587, and Perrot's troubles starting in late 1589 or early 1590. But in 1592 the difficulties for Perrot came to a head, while there is little evidence of the same sort of intensification for barrow. To the public at large and to those apt to buy *Groatsworth*, also, the case of Perrot would have been much more controversial (the queen was not pleased with the conduct of the case against him). Both readings were there, it seems. But if one of the two was the more topical and inflammatory, then it would have been the Perrot allegory. The Barrow allegory could serve as the screen. Its fox could be passed off as the old figure of hypocrisy or as some radical churchman, like Thomas Cartwright, and not Burghley. Such a screen, judging from his defense of himself in *Strange News*, was what Nashe had in mind with *Pierce*: "Let it be *Martin*, if you will," he said of his fox, "or some old dog that bites sorer than hee, who secretlie goes and seduceth country Swaines."[22]

---

[21] *State-Worthies* (1670), 511.

[22] Ed. McKerrow, 1:321. Missing the point, Donald J. McGinn, in *PMLA* 61 (1946): 431–53, accepted Nashe's fox as "perhaps Cartwright or Martin."

Appendix D

The Player-Patron

The scene in which Roberto is hired to write plays (lines 636–86), despite its promise, tells us little if anything about how Greene actually became a playwright. The Player-Patron is best understood to be a type of the successful actor of the day, who derived his wealth and smugness from an old-fashioned repertory and whose talent, though he himself thinks well of it, is, in Roberto's view, quite modest. The whole could be taken as an allegory of the arrival on the scene of the University Wits. It adapts into fiction (with dialogue) the content and attitude of its probable source, Nashe's preface to *Menaphon*, of 1589, reducing, in T. W. Baldwin's view, Nashe's no longer impoverished "company of taffaty fooles" down to the one successful actor.[1]

The Player's roles and plays, to the extent that we can identify them, seem intended to reflect the dramatic activity in general of the seventies and early eighties. There are one or two dramatized chivalric romances ("Delphrigus, and the King of Fairies"), a dramatized account of Hercules' labors, a late morality ("The High way to heaven"), several moral interludes about wit, and a scriptural comedy ("The Dialogue of Dives").

The account resembles other retrospectives during the time, similarly nostalgic and usually, like this one, patronizing or else openly critical. These start with Nashe's "company" in the preface to *Menaphon*, and include the players' scene in *More*, which appears to mention two of these plays, the offerings of Owlet's Men in *Histrio-mastix*, and the display of a rude sense of theater by Bottom and his mates in *A Midsummer Night's Dream*. Its criticism of the players— that they are proud, dress too well, are either rich or pretend to be— was common in complaints of preachers and turncoat dramatists beginning soon after the construction of the Theatre in 1576, and they can be found in Greene: in *Royal Exchange* (ent. 1590), in *Francesco's Fortunes*

---

[1] *Literary Genetics* (1959), 42. A much fuller discussion of the identity of this character will appear in *Studies in Philology* in 1994.

(1590), and in *A Quip for an Upstart Courtier* (1592).[2] The scene reflects a resentment at having to write for common players and, at the same time, at being paid so little compared to what the players make.

It seems probable that the portrait is a composite, suggesting a pattern of the highly successful actor, though traces of individuals may have been visible. Shakespeare, whom a number of scholars have recommended, was too young, as were Richard Burbage and Edward Alleyn.[3] E. K. Chambers, who thought the player largely fictional, allowed with some exasperation that it might be James Burbage.[4] The player's ability to build a windmill at his own cost may suggest Burbage: the Theatre, standing out there in the fields alongside three windmills, may have struck Londoners as a magnificent version of one. Burbage's acting, if such he did, would have been in the distant past, it seems. Robert Wilson, F. G. Fleay's suggestion, is not a bad guess, since he was quite famous, wrote plays, played, and performed extempore.[5] An interesting case could be made for Anthony Munday, Baldwin's suggestion, who wrote plays, was at one time an actor, and made an effort at extempore.[6] Munday is thought by some to be the original of the poet-player Posthaste who is treated with total contempt in *Histriomastix*. If it is in part Munday, then the portrait has to be playful, an inside joke, one of several, apparently, brought off in print by Chettle with his friend Munday in mind. Giorgio Melchiori has shown that Chettle and Munday together can be linked to the players' scene in *More*.[7] The portrait teases with its possibilities, delivering nothing firm.

---

[2] *Works*, ed. Grosart, 8:273, 133, 11:292.

[3] Shakespeare has been suggested by an anonymous author in *The New Monthly Magazine* 60, pt. 3 (1840): 297–304; Richard Simpson, *School of Shakspere*, 385–90; Alden Brooks, *Will Shakspere: Factotum and Agent* (New York: Round Table, 1937), 115–27, and *Will Shakspere and the Dyer's Hand* (New York: C. Scribner's, 1943), 55–62; M. C. Bradbrook, *Shakespeare Survey* 15 (1962): 65–66, and *Rise of the Common Player* (1962), 85–86; and A. L. Rowse, *Shakespeare the Man* (New York: Harper & Row, 1973), 60. All agree the portrait is more or less a distortion. Alleyn was suggested by Arthur Acheson, in *Shakespeare's Lost Years* (1920), 101–5.

[4] *Eliz. Stage*, 1:377 n.

[5] *Biog. Chron.*, 278–83. Fleay's idea was rejected by Chambers, *Eliz. Stage*, 2:349, and Irene Mann, in her unpubl. diss. "The Text of the Plays of Robert Wilson" (Univ. of Virginia, 1942), 32–33.

[6] *Literary Genetics* (1959), 41–45. Baldwin appears to have grown less confident, arguing (517) that the account is "for the most part fictional," even that it could be one of the Dutton brothers, John and Laurence, in charge at various times of Queen's divisions in 1589–92.

[7] *Le Forme del Teatro* 3 (1984): 59–94.

Appendix E

"thou famous gracer of Tragedians"

By near universal consent the first playwright addressed in the famous letter (lines 884–916) is Christopher Marlowe. The curious word *gracer*, which has no earlier recorded history, may have sounded like a slurred or hurried *Cristopher* (*grace* = *Chris*). But there are other reasons why *grace* itself might have been identified with Marlowe.[1] Marlowe is warned that, as Greene's suffering can testify, atheism provokes God's punishment. After suggesting that Machiavelli is the source of that atheism, "Greene" challenges the doctrine that power in rulers ought to be purely selfish and immoral and proceeds to offer as an object lesson the troubles of Machiavelli's own life and death. Thus put, the warning amounted to a charge of atheism, and a serious one, since it gave the impression of coming from one who knew Marlowe personally and intimately ("my friend"), and one who has shared not merely his occupation but, so it is claimed, his radical views as well. Here is a good reason, perhaps the reason, *Groatsworth* created such a stir. One could be imprisoned and tortured and then hanged or burnt for unorthodox attitudes in matters of religion. Marlowe was one of the "one or two" Chettle tells us took offense at the pamphlet and accused Chettle of writing it, the one whom Chettle says he did not know and had no wish to know, though he admired his learning. That which Chettle admits having "stroke out," which Greene must have "in some displeasure writ," because "to publish it, was intollerable," may have been something specifically

---

[1] Cf. Prol. to *Faustus*: "So much he profits in divinity, / The fruitful plot of scholarism graced, / That shortly he was graced with Doctor's name" (lines 6–8, ed. Bowers [1981]); Prol. to *Jew of Malta*: "I crave but this, Grace him as he deserves, / And let him not be entertain'd the worse / Because he favours me" (lines 33–35, ed. Bowers). At Cambridge *grace* was permission to proceed to the degree. In his dissertation (but not elsewhere) C. E. Sanders argues that Thomas Watson, not Marlowe, is addressed (*Abstracts of Theses: Humanistic Series*, Univ. of Chicago, 5 [1928], 487–91).

and outrageously blasphemous.[2] One can inflict greater damage by suggesting that something even more alarming has been suppressed. For this reason, no doubt, and for the enlightenment it might bring to posterity, Frederick S. Boas, with all due respect to Chettle's scruples, wished he had simply let the "intollerable" details stand.[3]

Needless to say, the motive behind the passage has been impugned. That the warning is effectively hostile seems impossible to deny. John H. Ingram put it "amid the blackest records of human infamy."[4] We might also incline to see it as impertinent, since we assume, with Una Ellis-Fermor, that Marlowe knew well enough how to meet the terrors of the human soul, even better "than Greene could have learned had his life been indefinitely prolonged."[5] We might allow that the malice is unconscious, because otherwise it is unthinkable that Greene or Chettle should address Marlowe in such a way. (Ingram suspected Greene of leaving the manuscript with some bookseller as security for a small advance with instructions not to publish it until after his death.) No doubt Greene's attitude toward Marlowe was, as Chettle would know, complex, admiration mixed with resentment, the admiration reflected in his desire to identify with Marlowe (scholar-playwrights, friends, and fellow atheists), the resentment stemming from Marlowe's manifest superiority in playmaking and, perhaps, Marlowe's indifference to him.

Every reference in print to Marlowe by Greene, those we recognize and those we suspect, is hostile. In the first, the preface to *Perimedes* (1588), Greene defends himself against criticism that he could not make his "verses jet upon the stage in tragicall buskins, everie worde filling the mouth like the faburden of Bo-Bell, daring God out of heaven with that Atheist *Tamburlan*"—a clear attack upon Marlowe (the creation standing for its creator), and the first use of the term "atheist" with Marlowe.[6] Greene is thought to have failed with *Alphonsus* in an effort to imitate *Tamburlaine*. Other Greene plays there-

---

[2] *Kind-Hartes Dreame*, ed. Harrison, 5–6. It may have had to do with his sexual orientation. "Pederastice [was] a kinde of harlatry, not to be recited" (Harvey, *A New Letter*, 1593 [*Works*, ed. Grosart], 1:290). Russell Fraser imagines that Chettle left out Marlowe's remark about all being fools who didn't love boys or tobacco (*Young Shakespeare* [New York: Columbia Univ. Press, 1988], 143).

[3] *Christopher Marlowe: A Biographical and Critical Study* (Oxford: Clarendon Press, 1940), 240–41.

[4] *Christopher Marlowe and His Associates* (London: Grant Richards, 1904), 194–95.

[5] *Christopher Marlowe* (1927; repr. Hamden, CT: Archon Books, 1967), 162.

[6] *Works*, ed. Grosart, 7:7–8.

after appear to have exploited without much success motifs that Marlowe made popular. Envy, therefore, the color of his name, has been taken to be his main attitude, and part of his nature, too, since it shifts in the letter from Marlowe to the recently-successful Shakespeare. The motive here, says John Bakeless, is spite taking the form of piety, "as spite is very likely to do, . . . masking itself as a sincere desire for the sinner's repentance."[7] In Ellis-Fermor's view, Greene's voice comes to us through a "tangle of fear, malice, hysterical exultation and equally hysterical self-condemnation."[8] Some have taken the motive to be pure: René Pruvost thought it sincere; Boas heard, not the anger of 1588 or envy, but sorrow; Philip Henderson heard "a friend in the sincerity of his heart."[9] Though the evidence suggests otherwise, the two may have been friends, which would account for the solicitude. But unless the two were hopelessly out of touch, nothing could justify or excuse so public an expression of it.

The charge in late 1592, as we have seen, whatever its motives, was not new. Marlowe's reputation as a free-thinker, based on his public statements, his plays, and the company he kept, was apparently widespread, and his world was one in which any serious questioning of received views could be labeled atheistic.[10] There is thus little consensus as to the value of the passage as evidence of what Marlowe actually thought. To Ellis-Fermor it "does not sound like the writing of a man who knew what were Marlowe's deepest interests or understood his most representative thought" (which would certainly be true of Chettle), and yet to Paul H. Kocher it "seems to indicate that Greene knew [Marlowe's] beliefs at first hand."[11] It is the only clear evidence that Marlowe was an atheist in the modern sense of the word, and accordingly deserves a place in discussions of the nature of that atheism, called by George T. Buckley "one of the most involved and baffling problems in the whole course of sixteenth-century literature."[12] Despite this apparent confession, no one assumes that Greene's atheism ran deep.

---

[7] *Tragicall History of Christopher Marlowe* (Cambridge, MA: Harvard Univ. Press, 1942), 1:97.

[8] *Marlowe*, 160.

[9] *Robert Greene et ses Romans*, 517; *Marlowe*, 238; *Christopher Marlowe* (1952; repr. New York: Barnes & Noble, 1974), 37.

[10] Bakeless lists contemporary evidence as to Marlowe's unorthodox religious views, in *Marlowe*, vol. 1, chap. v.

[11] *Marlowe*, 162; *Christopher Marlowe: A Study of His Thought, Learning, and Character* (Chapel Hill: Univ. of North Carolina Press, 1946), 78.

[12] *Atheism in the English Renaissance* (1932; repr. New York: Russell & Russell, 1965), 121.

The attribution of Marlowe's beliefs in part reflects the view then common that Machiavelli was "the greatest single source of atheism in Western Europe."[13] He was thought to have led large numbers of Englishmen astray. The author may have had in mind a more specific connection as well, since Marlowe probably read Machiavelli at Cambridge. Harvey tells us he was being read there by "an odd crewe or tooe" in 1579, a year before Marlowe arrived.[14] In any case, Marlowe's plays have suggested to many that he was absorbed with Machiavelli, that he had, in Edward Meyer's words, "studied Machiavelli with a vengeance."[15] Machiavelli, recently come from France, serves as the Prologue to *The Jew of Malta* and declares that he "count[s] Religion but a childish Toy, / And hold[s] there is no sinne but Ignorance."[16] The maxim offered here as Machiavelli's basic tenet—"*Sic volo, sic iubeo*"—"underlies the program of virtually every one of [Marlowe's] great domineering figures" (Kocher); and the conclusion here, that it would lead to the destruction of life, correctly diagnoses "the power politics practiced by Marlowe's supermen and [supplies] a remarkable forecast of the atomic age" (Henderson).[17] Even the style of this address might suggest Marlowe. So it did for Boas, for whom it caught "the secret of [Marlowe's] soaring and sombre rhetoric in this vision of the final catastrophe of mankind."[18]

Groatsworth's distorted version of Machiavelli's life, that he lived in fear, was a murderer, and died a suicide, was probably current, though the evidence is limited. No exact source has turned up. Meyer rejects as having "absolutely no authority" Richard Simpson's statement that "in Greene's day Machiavelli was generally believed in England to have perished by his own hand." It was "Greene's own foul fabrication," Meyer fumed, just what "was to be expected from this blaggard liar, puking forth his putrid surfeit from a drunkard's

---

[13] *Atheism in the English Renaissance*, 31.

[14] *Works*, ed. Grosart, 1:138.

[15] *Machiavelli and the Elizabethan Drama* (1897; repr. New York: B. Franklin, 1969), 33.

[16] Lines 14–15 (ed. Bowers [1981]).

[17] Kocher, 180, and see 211; Henderson, 36–37.

[18] *Marlowe*, 239. For years the "brocher [broker] of this Diabolicall Atheisme" was misread. Malone took "brother" of later Qq (which he thought should be "breather") to be Francis Kett, the unitarian burnt in Norwich in 1589, who had been at Cambridge (*Plays and Poems of William Shakspeare*, ed. Boswell [1821], 2:303). Others took his position. In 1874 Richard Simpson showed that the "brocher" is Machiavelli himself (*Academy*, 21 March, 309–10), although "brother" continued to puzzle some.

death-bed!"[19] For the view of Machiavelli as atheist, Mario Praz considered that Gentillet, whose *Contre-Machiavel* had been available in England since 1576, simply gave the "finishing touch" to a dark picture "the Catholic clergy had been elaborating for half a century." Praz traced the account of the death, if not the suicide, to the Jesuit Raynaud: "*blasphemans evomuit reprobum spiritum.*"[20]

The address alludes as much to morals as to doctrine, to Epicureanism as to Machiavellianism, the former, not the latter, applying to all three friends ("Despise drunkennes. . . . Flie lust. . . . Abhorre those Epicures. . . ."). Greene had linked the two attitudes in the epistle to *The Second Part of Cony-Catching* late in 1591.[21] The chapter in Thomas Beard's *Theatre of God's Judgements*, in 1597, that gives the account of Marlowe's death is called "Of Epicures and Atheists" (Chap. xxv), and Francis Meres, in *Palladis Tamia*, in 1598, compares Marlowe with the French poet Jodelle "for his Epicurisme and Atheisme" (a combination Meres uses three times).[22] Marlowe appeared before the Court of the Star Chamber to be questioned as to his religious views on 20 May 1593, and died in a tavern brawl on 30 May. *Groatsworth*'s words, then, as Boas observed, were to be "more luridly prophetic" than could have been foreseen.[23]

---

[19] Simpson, *Academy*, 309, also in *Shakspere Allusion-Books* (1874), 1:xlviii; *Machiavelli and the Elizabethan Drama*, 69.

[20] "Machiavelli and the Elizabethans," *Proceedings of the British Academy* 14 (1928): 34, rev. as *The Flaming Heart* (New York: Doubleday, 1958), 129–30. For Gentillet in Simon Patericke's trans., *Discourse upon the Means of Well Governing* (1602), on Machiavelli's atheism and avarice, see the preface and 92–99.

[21] *Works*, ed. Grosart, 10:73.

[22] Facs. (1973), 286ᵛ, which cites Beard. Marlowe's sexual proclivities could have been treated under the idea of Epicureanism. Cf. Patericke's trans. of Gentillet (*Discourse*, 102): "[of] the sect of the Epicures, which were gluttons, drunkards, and whoremongers, which consitituted their sovereigne felicitie in carnall pleasures, wherein they wallowed like brute beasts. Out of this schoole, *Machiavell* and the *Machiavelists* come, caring for nothing but their pleasures."

[23] *Marlowe*, 239.

Appendix F

"yong Juvenall"

These lines (917–26) are almost certainly addressed to Nashe, not Thomas Lodge. Thomas Tyrwhitt, who first noticed the passage some time before 1773, thought Lodge was addressed. When Richard Farmer, soon after, suggested Nashe, Edmond Malone reacted by declaring for Lodge, and he was followed in time by Alexander Dyce, F. G. Fleay, Churton Collins and others. In 1874, Richard Simpson, to support a recommendation made that year by Howard Staunton, outlined the case for Nashe, one then reprinted with approval by C. M. Ingleby and by Grosart in his edition of Greene. Thereafter, with varying degrees of certainty, Edmund W. Gosse, C. M. Gayley, R. B. McKerrow, and E. K. Chambers came out for Nashe. In 1967, just when agreement seemed unanimous and the issue settled, Philip Drew, after surveying evidence for both candidates, found the *"positive* facts" to favor Lodge and the arguments against him to be "all circumstantial and even taken together . . . inconclusive," though he did allow that a "respectable case" could be made out for Nashe on impressionistic grounds. The case for Nashe is very strong.[1]

Since Nashe was born in 1567, Lodge probably in 1557, and

---

[1] Tyrwhitt, in *Plays and Poems of Shakspeare,* ed. Boswell (1821), 18:551–52; Malone and Farmer, in ibid., 2:307; Dyce, *Dramatic Works of Greene* (1831), lxxx, n.; *Dramatic and Poetical Works of Greene & Peele* (1861), 60 n.; Fleay, *William Shakespeare* (1886), 17; *Biog. Chron.* (1891), 1:260–62; Collins, ed., *Plays & Poems* (1905), 1:138–39 n.; Simpson, *Academy,* 11 April 1874, 400; *School of Shakspere* (1878), 381–83; Staunton, *Athenaeum,* 21 March 1874, 391; Ingleby, *Shakspere Allusion-Books* (1874), 1:vi–viii, xxxvii–xli; Grosart, ed., *Works,* 1:lvii–lxv; Gosse, *Works of Lodge* (1883), 1:29–30; Gayley, *Repr. Engl. Com.* (1903), 1:423–26; McKerrow, ed., *Nashe,* 5:142–44; Chambers, *Eliz. Stage,* 3:326; Drew, *Studies in English Literature* 7 (1967): 55–66, whose argument should be considered on its own. C. J. Sisson thought it "probably Lodge," in *Thomas Lodge,* 103; Pruvost (*Greene,* 521–24) thought Nashe. That Chettle defends Nashe against a charge of having written *Groatsworth,* used by Malone and others against an allusion to him here, means little. The allusion to him may have been overlooked or considered purposely planted to cover his responsibility.

Greene in 1558, "yong *Juvenall*" and "Sweet boy" would seem more appropriate for Nashe. His youthfulness must have been pronounced in 1592–93; to Janet E. Biller it is one of the two *foci* in Harvey's *Four Letters* (the other is the exaggeration in Nashe's style).[2] In the second letter, dated 5 September, Harvey calls "his [Greene's] fellow-writer, a proper yong man, if advised in time."[3] Here *fellow-writer* and *advised* also link Nashe with our passage, where *advise* and *advisde* occur, and may have suggested it to Chettle. In his third letter, dated 8 and 9 September, with obvious reference to Nashe, Harvey lists certain "Gyants in conceit, and Pigmeis in performance: yong Phaetons, younge Icary, young Chorœbi, and I shall say young Babingtons." In *Pierce's Supererogation* (1593) Harvey calls Nashe "young Apuleius" twelve times, calls him "great Captaine of the boyes," "young Asse," "colt" (twice), "young Curtisan," "young Poet," "Tomboy," "young man," "puppy," and refers to his "greene, and wild youth," to his "unlearned, or unexpert youth." Nashe is a "youngman of the greenest springe, as beardles in judgement, as in face; and as Penniles in witt, as in purse," and of a "beardless chinne." And in *A New Letter of Notable Contents* (1593) Harvey calls him "young Apuleius" again and refers to "the shallow brest of inconsiderate youth."[4] Collins would remove the difficulty by making "yong" in *Groatsworth* mean "modern"; but if the person meant were not young at all, as Lodge was not, then the epithet, being taken as ironic, would distract from the letter's serious business. Greene uses such a joke in *James IV* when he has Slipper describe himself as a "young stripling of the age of thirty years."[5]

Contemporaries appear to have thought "yong *Juvenall*" referred to Nashe. In *Palladis Tamia* (1598), Francis Meres, who tended to hand on whatever was going around, calls Nashe "gallant young Juvenall" (and "sweete Tom" as well). (In 1598 Nashe would have been just over thirty.) We should notice, while with Meres, another comment which appears to connect Nashe with our passage (the word *libertie* and the hostility toward the Harveys): "As Eupolis of Athens used great libertie in taxing the vices of men: so doth Thomas Nash, witnesse the broode of the Harveys!"[6] In III.i of *Love's Labour's Lost*,

---

[2] "Gabriel Harvey's *Foure Letters* (1592)," lxxiv.

[3] *Foure Letters*, ed. Harrison, 21.

[4] *Foure Letters*, ed. Harrison, 43; *Works*, ed. Grosart, *Super.*, 2:39–40, 59, 119, 121, 265, 50, 242, 59, 76, 239, 91, 92, 229, 265, 273, 96, 274, 75, 246; *New Letter*, 1:274, 286.

[5] I.ii.58–59 (ed. Sanders).

[6] Facs. (1973), 286^v, 286^r.

usually dated late 1593, Armado's addressing Moth as "tender juvenal" has been taken by most to suggest that something of Nashe is in Moth (*Moth* is an anagram of *Thom*), to be a variation of this epithet (with the same duplication of *young*, since *tender* meant *young*), and to recall *Groatsworth*. Richard David judges to be "overwhelming" the "cumulative effect" of parallels in that play with the Nashe-Harvey quarrel.[7] Moreover, such comparisons were frequent at the time in efforts to describe Nashe's remarkable style. Harvey calls him a "brave Columbus of tearmes," and over and again compares him with Aretino and Rabelais, Elderton and Tarlton. For Lodge he was the "true English Aretine."[8]

The chief argument for Nashe centers on style: his expression is distinctive, startling and vicious, whereas Lodge's, by comparison, is not nearly so interesting. It has little bite. We have ample evidence throughout Harvey, who was obsessed with Nashe's style, that Nashe would have been recognized as a "byting Satyrist." As Grosart put it, he "acquired a sudden and a lasting reputation as *the first and most formidable satirist of his epoch*."[9] This style they knew not so much from *The Anatomy of Absurdity* (1590), which rarely displays it, as from *An Almond for a Parrot* (1590), presumably other Marprelate tracts as well, from introductory epistles, and perhaps from plays now lost. *Pierce Penniless* was entered on 8 August and published early in September. Very little in Lodge's prose or in his satiric poetry, which means *A Fig for Momus*, published in 1595 though possibly available beforehand, could have been, or could now be, considered Juvenalian, though he may have been thought of as a satirist in 1592. *An Alarm Against Usurers* (1584) and *Catharos* (1591) are in a satiric mode, and he has a poem in *Scilla's Metamorphosis* (1589) called "the Discontented Satyre," which is not very satiric. What we see they could see as well, that Nashe's style is more obviously satiric, more consistently so, and more nearly suggestive of Juvenal. It is true that Meres lists Lodge and not Nashe among those "best for Satyre," but he probably thought of satire in its commonly accepted academic sense as verse

---

[7] In his Arden edition (1956), xxxix–xliv; see also Charles Nicholl, *A Cup of News: The Life of Thomas Nashe* (London: Routledge & Kegan Paul, 1984), 212–20.

[8] Harvey, *Works*, ed. Grosart, 2:45; *Foure Letters*, ed. Harrison, 51, 52, 53, 66, 67; *Works*, ed. Grosart, 1:272; Lodge, *Wits Misery* (1596), in *Works* (ed. 1883), 4:63.

[9] Ed., Greene, *Works*, 1:lxii.

(he lists only poets), and *A Fig* (1595) had by that time been printed.[10] It may also be, given the coding tactics at the time, that *byting*
hints at Nashe through *gnashing*, even as it nicely suggests *carpenda* of
the typical academic definition of *satira*.[11] Harvey talks about
Nashe's "gnashing language," calls him "Gnasharduccio" and his
style "meere Nashery" and "gnashing Hell," and asks "what dowty
yoonker [youth] may next gnash with his teeth?"[12]

The case for Lodge relies partly on the existence of a comedy, *A
Looking Glass for London and England*, by Lodge and Greene, attributed to them in its entry of 1594 and on title pages of 1594 and after.
But according to present thinking this play was at least two years old
in 1592, and Lodge is generally thought to have sailed with Caven-
dish in August 1591.[13] The word *lastly* may have meant, in the
strictest sense, "the most recently," as Philip Drew, looking at the
one other quotation in the *OED*, suggests, and not simply "recently"
(*OED*'s definition) or "lately" as some have defined it. Drew reads
"that lastly with mee together writ a Comedie" in two ways which
allow for a play two years old: (1) who was the last collaborator I had,
and (2) who has not written a comedy since he wrote one with me.
For Lodge to be meant, we must assume that Greene had no collaborator for two years, which seems rather long, or that an allusion to an
older play, one which certainly had been successful, would still be
meaningful. Our natural reaction, based on *lastly* and the context as
a whole, is to infer that the play was written recently. Moreover, in
the conclusion of *Scilla's Metamorphosis*, in 1589, Lodge had announced his intention of writing no more for the public theaters, at
least such is how we interpret these lines:

> And then by oath he bound me
> To write no more, of that whence shame dooth grow:

---

[10] *Palladis Tamia*, facs. (1973), 283[v]. McKerrow thought that "'satire'
generally, if not always, meant verse," and therefore thought it "not impossible
that the 'lines' may have been some verse lampoons against Richard Harvey
which had been circulated by Nashe in manuscript" (ed., *Nashe*, 5:142–44).
Anthony à Wood thought Lodge's reputation as a satirist quite high: "After he
[Lodge] had taken one Degree in Arts, and had spent some time in exercising his
fancy among the Poets in the great City, he was esteemed (not *Jos. Hall* of
Emanuel Coll. in *Cambridge* excepted) the best for Satyr among *English* Men."
(*Athenae Oxonienses*, 1691).

[11] Drant called it a "carpyng kynd of verse," quoted by Mary Claire Randolph
in *Notes and Queries* 180 (1941): 416.

[12] *Works*, 2:231, 18, 234; *Foure Letters*, ed. Harrison, 47, 43.

[13] See Waldo F. McNeir, "The Date of *A Looking Glass for London*," *Notes
and Queries* 200 (1955): 282–83.

Or tie my pen to *Penie-knaves* delight,
But live with fame, and so for fame to wright.[14]

Why should anyone advise Lodge to do that which he already knows
he should do and, by sailing away, has in effect done?

Efforts to find a collaboration with Nashe have not been very
successful. *A Knack to Know a Knave*, the leading serious candidate
(Richard Simpson, G. M. Gayley), was described by Henslowe as
"ne" in June 1592, a summer in which Nashe and Greene did spend
some time together.[15] But to many the play reflects nothing of
Nashe's style. E. H. Miller, Donald J. McGinn, and Charles Nicholl
have argued that the most appropriate sense of "Comedie" here is
that of a diverting situation in prose, a sense used elsewhere by
Greene. Miller and Nicholl offer *The Defence of Cony-Catching*, entered 21 April 1592, and McGinn *A Quip for an Upstart Courtier*,
entered 20 July 1592.[16] G. R. Hibbard's reaction is appropriate: the
whole point of the passage demands that *Comedie* be given a dramatic
interpretation. Greene advises *"those Gentlemen his Quondam acquaintance, that spend their wits in making plaies"* that they should no longer
do so. They will be mistreated; it is the actors, not they, who draw
wealth and fame from their plays.[17] We do not know what "Comedie" the two collaborated on in the spring or summer of 1592,
assuming the passage was composed during this time and not some
time before. Of some relevance ought to be a comment Nashe makes
when, in *Have With You* (1596), he contrasts his talents with
Greene's: "while hee liv'd (as some Stationers can witnes with me)
hee subscribing to me in any thing but plotting Plaies, wherein he was

---

[14] *Works* (ed. 1883), 1:28.

[15] Hanspeter Born, *The Rare Wit and the Rude Groom: The Authorship of "A Knack to Know a Knave" in Relation to Greene, Nashe & Shakespeare* (Bern: Francke, [1971]), 57–65, thinks *Knave* "the most plausible candidate"; Paul E. Bennett's 1952 diss. edition (Univ. of Penn.; *DA*, 13 [1953], 226), "tentatively" assigns it to Greene and rejects the possibility of Nashe; G. R. Hibbard, in *Thomas Nashe* (Cambridge, MA: Harvard Univ. Press, 1962), rejects the idea (86); G. R. Proudfoot's 1961 Oxford diss. edition finds it "not impossible" (lxii; in Born, 64 n.). Gosse suggested *George a Greene*; J. M. Robertson, in *State of Shakespeare Study* (London: Routledge & Sons, 1931) *Two Gentlemen of Verona* (162–64).

[16] Miller, "The Relationship of Robert Greene and Thomas Nashe," *Philological Quarterly* 33 (1954): 358–62; McGinn, "A Quip for Tom Nashe," *Studies in English Renaissance Drama*, ed. Josephine W. Bennet, et al. (New York: New York Univ. Press, 1959), 172–88; Nicholl, *Cup of News*, 125–30.

[17] *Thomas Nashe*, 255.

his crafts master."[18] This Drew takes "on its face" to be evidence
that "Greene had refused to allow Nashe to work with him on a
play." It could just as easily mean that Greene was simply *better* at
writing plays (his plays sold better than Nashe's), or, just possibly,
that he was better at supplying the plots of plays (the basic situations,
as they knew from what plays sold). Both Lodge and Nashe are on
Meres' list as "best for Comedy amongst us."[19]

The "Schollers vexed with sharpe lines" must be the Harveys,
between whom and Nashe there had been tensions for well over two
years. In *Plain Perceval* in 1589 Richard Harvey attacked the
anti-Martinists, which means Nashe's friends, Greene among them,
and almost certainly Nashe as well; in an epistle to his *Lamb of God*
in 1590 he attacked Nashe by name for presuming to be an expert on
literary affairs in his 1589 preface to Greene's *Menaphon*. There may
have been "intermediate links" (McKerrow) in the quarrel, but for a
two-year period nothing survives. Greene probably saw before publication the sustained attack on Richard in *Pierce*. Quite possibly this
advice reflects Greene's own regret for having attacked the Harveys,
an attack that may even have occurred at the urging of Nashe, in *A
Quip* in July, or else Chettle's awareness of Greene's regret. Greene
does seem to have had a change of heart (he seems not have known
that Gabriel's brother John died just before the publication of *Quip*),
since he, both Harvey and Nashe say, removed the offending passage
from *Quip* after the first editions. McKerrow's observation that
"Lodge had, so far as one knows, never had a quarrel with any
scholars" can be misleading. As Drew reminds us, Lodge had been at
one time in open conflict with Stephen Gosson. Gosson's *School of
Abuse* (which explains "Schollers"?) was printed in 1579, Lodge's
Reply, which appears to have been suppressed, probably in 1579–80,
Gosson's *Plays Confuted*, which carries on the conflict, in 1582, and
Lodge's epistle to *An Alarum for Usurers* in 1584. Portions of the
Reply and the epistle do attack Gosson in ways which should be
described as personal. But this was a quarrel of the early eighties. The
quarrel with the Harveys, which had become serious by the end of the
summer of 1592, was *the* literary event of the early nineties. *Groatsworth's* advice, whoever wrote it, is conciliatory, affectionately patronizing, not what one would expect for Lodge, who had been around
and could handle his own affairs. In E. H. Miller's opinion Nashe
"probably resented this gratuitous advice which, despite the praise at

---

[18] *Works*, ed. McKerrow, 3:132.
[19] *Palladis Tamia*, facs. (1973), 283^v.

the beginning of the passage, aligns Greene with 'Juvenal's' critics."[20]
It is also consistent, as Chettle would have known, with an impression
otherwise available in Greene's works of a reluctance to name names.

Three other places in texts after *Groatsworth* suggest Nashe. In
Kind-Heart's Dream, entered on 8 December 1592, Chettle has the
ghost of Greene excite Nashe to revenge with these words: "And
albeit I would disswade thee from more invectives against such thy
adversaries (for peace is nowe all my plea) yet I know thou wilt
returne answere...."[21] Chettle had no reason to supply the qualifi-
cation at all ("And ... albeit"), anxious as he was to have Nashe
continue the battle, unless he remembered, and knew others remembered, what was supposed to be Greene's advice in the letter. In
Pierce's Supererogation (1593), Harvey seems to echo the attack: "yet
Thomas Nashe might have beene advised, and in pollicy have spared
them [meaning himself], that in compassion favoured him."[22] And
in *A Knight's Conjuring* (1607), Thomas Dekker gathers into a vision
of the underworld the four playwrights of this letter: "whil'st *Marlow*,
Greene, and *Peele* had got under the shades of a large *vyne*, laughing
to see *Nash* (that was but newly come to their Colledge,) still haunted
with the sharpe and *Satyricall spirit* that followed him heere upon
earth." Moreover, Nashe is asked "how Poets and Players agreed
now," which is exactly the concern of *Groatsworth*'s letter. As if to
lock in the connection, Dekker has none other than Chettle himself
arrive, "sweating and blowing, by reason of his fatnes, to welcome
whom, because hee was of olde acquaintance, all rose up...."[23]

---

[20] "Relationship of Greene and Nashe," 358.

[21] Ed. Harrison, 36.

[22] Ed. Grosart, 2:80.

[23] K4^v-L1^v. Biller (ed. 1969, p. 72a) takes Sonnet IIII (on 88 in *Foure Letters*,
ed. Harrison), published originally after the third letter, to refer to *Groatsworth*'s
letter: "The jolly Fly dispatch'd his silly selfe; / What Storyes quaint of many a
douty Fly, / That read a Lecture to the ventrous Elfe?" If this reading is correct,
then here, published with a letter dated 8 and 9 September, would be an instance
of Harvey knowing *Groatsworth* before it is registered on 20 September. The elf,
however, is more likely to be Greene (Robin Goodfellow) and the fly Nashe
(*Thom* = *Moth*), and the reference ("Lecture") thus to *Anatomy* (1:16): "[to
those] who with Greene Colours, seeke to garnish such Gorgonlike shapes [wom-
en]."

Appendix G

"upstart Crow"

Our conception of Shakespeare's early career long depended on what we made of the "upstart Crow" passage (lines 932–43). It is the first text after his own works to command attention, and the most significant contemporary comment on him after Ben Jonson's poem in the First Folio. It can never be "too minutely investigated" (J. O. Halliwell-Phillipps); it "needs slow digestion" (Anthony Burgess).[1] We turn to it again and again, trying to get it right, and have as a consequence produced on it a small library of serious comment. It would be useless in this survey, as we have elsewhere, to insist on a distinction between Greene and a Chettle trying to pass himself off as Greene. If Chettle wrote it, he had to have presented attitudes either widely believed to be Greene's or else to be close enough. Its views on actors in general could have been inferred directly from what Greene (and Nashe) had put into print.

The commentators have sought primarily to establish the precise nature of the charge against Shakespeare. As an actor, he shares the blame for having forsaken one now sick and destitute, whose services he once readily exploited. And he, like them, is susceptible to a charge of pride because actors, who can say only what those more worthy than they put into their mouths, enjoy a fame and wealth undeserved. But why is Shakespeare singled out? Is it solely that he represents a more outrageous order of pride than the others in that he, a mere uneducated player, has ventured to write plays himself? Or is the charge that he, unlike the others, has appropriated the plays of Greene and friends to his own use in an unfair or dishonest manner? Is Shakespeare being accused of plagiarism? Most now take the

---

[1] *Life of William Shakespeare* (1848; repr. New York: AMS, 1973), 145; *Shakespeare* (New York: Alfred A. Knopf, 1970), 108. C. E. Sanders thought the "Crow" Marlowe (*Abstracts of Theses*, Univ. of Chicago 5 [1928]: 489); W. H. Chapman thought it Will Kemp or Robert Wilson (*William Shakespeare* [1912], 26); Winifred Frazer has suggested Kemp (*PMLA* 108 [1993]: 335).

charge to be impudence, but few would deny that the passage puzzles. Something ambiguous hovers at the center of its expression just at the point where we might hope, in this first certain allusion to Shakespeare in London, for a clue to his early practice as a dramatist. It was largely on the basis of one reading of this outburst that for over a century scholars thought that several of Shakespeare's early plays were revisions of plays by others.

Edmond Malone set down the interpretation which long prevailed. The "visible *inequality*" of the second and third *Henry VI* plays, and perhaps Richard Farmer's skepticism as to Shakespeare's ability to write such plays, convinced him that Shakespeare had revised plays by Greene and Peele preserved in the quartos as *The First Part of the Contention Betwixt the Two Famous Houses of York and Lancaster* (pr. in 1594) and *The True Tragedy of Richard Duke of York* (pr. in 1595). Malone was aware that Thomas Tyrwhitt, who discovered the allusion and published it in the 1778 Steevens-Johnson edition of the plays, thought it confirmed Shakespeare's authorship of *3 Henry VI*; and he apparently assented to that interpretation at first, in his *Attempt to Ascertain the Order in which the Plays of Shakspeare Were Written* (1778). But by 1787, in his *Dissertation on the Three Parts of "King Henry VI"*, he had changed his mind. This attack, he now claimed, gave "decisive support" to his hypothesis, indeed "first suggested" it to him, and became "the chief hinge" of his argument.

> [Greene] therefore, in direct terms, charges [Shakespeare] with having acted like the crow in the fable, *beautified himself with their feathers*; in other words, with having acquired fame *furtivis coloribus*, by new-modelling a work originally produced by them, and wishing to depreciate our author, he very naturally quotes a line from one of the pieces which Shakespeare had thus *re-written*.

The word *bombast,* meaning "to amplify and swell out," described exactly what Greene was suggesting Shakespeare did to the work of others.[2]

On Malone's authority scholars undertook to discover evidence of revision, especially of plays by Greene and friends, and the common biography took it as an article of faith that so Shakespeare began his

---

[2] In *Plays and Poems of William Shakspeare*, ed. Boswell (1821), 18:570–71; *Dissertation* (1787), 19–22; *Plays and Poems of William Shakspeare*, ed. Malone (1790), 6:397–99. Tyrwhitt's notice is in Steevens' *Plays of William Shakspeare* (1778), 6:565–66; ed. Boswell (1821), 18:551–52. Malone mentions the Tyrwhitt discovery in his *Attempt*, in *Plays*, ed. Steevens (1778), 1:277–78, 283, and discusses the passage in the 1790 version, pt. 1, 1:272–80; ed. Boswell (1821), 2:302–15.

career. "This passage from Greene," J. S. Smart complained in 1928, with reference to Malone's interpretation, "has had such a devastating effect on Shakespearian study that we cannot but wish it had never been written or never discovered." It was the sapling, to W. W. Greg in 1942, from which "sprang a whole jungle of critical and biographical error."[3]

Some did question Malone's reading early on: a writer in *The Edinburgh Review* in 1840, Charles Knight in 1843, Thomas Kenny in 1864, Richard Simpson in 1874, and C. F. Tucker Brooke in 1912, the last of whom thought an accusation of plagiarism at a time when theatrical companies owned plays outright would have been absurd.[4] That borrowing of some kind was intended, however, was generally taken for granted until Peter Alexander (1929), inspired by Smart (1928), concluded from a detailed study of the texts that the *Contention* and *True Tragedy* are not early versions of *2* and *3 Henry VI* but are, instead, memorial reports of Shakespeare's plays produced by actors who had taken minor parts.[5] This being the case, similar assumptions about other early plays, such as *Titus* and *The Shrew*, had to be altered. Moreover, in the Smart-Alexander view the traditional construction of the words of this passage was wrong.

First, "upstart Crow, beautified with our feathers" means no more than that Shakespeare is an actor and thus relies for profit and applause on the lines of writers such as Greene and his friends. The phrase simply repeats the foregoing two equivalent phrases: "those Puppets . . . that spake from our mouths, those Anticks garnisht in our colours." It was a grievance long standing with Greene, and he had clearly used the image with this meaning in 1590 in *Francesco's Fortunes*:

why *Roscius*, art thou proud with *Esops* Crow, being pranct with the glorie of others feathers? of they selfe thou canst say nothing, and if the Cobler hath taught thee to say *Ave Caesar*, disdain not thy tutor, because thou pratest in a Kings chamber.[6]

---

[3] *Shakespeare: Truth and Tradition* (repr. Oxford: Clarendon Press, 1966), 167; *Editorial Problem in Shakespeare* (Oxford: Clarendon Press), 52.

[4] (July, 1840): 7:474; *Comedies, Histories, Tragedies* (1842–44), 7:75, 74; *The Life and Genius of Shakespeare* (London), 288–89; *Academy*, 4 April 1874, 368; *The Authorship of the Second and Third Parts of "King Henry VI"* (New Haven: Yale Univ. Press, 1912), 190.

[5] *Shakespeare's "Henry VI" and "Richard III"* (Cambridge: University Press), 40–50; *Shakespeare: Truth and Traditon*, 163–69. Chambers may have arrived independently at the same reading, in *William Shakespeare* (Oxford: Clarendon Press, 1930), 1:217.

[6] *Works*, ed. Grosart, 8:132.

Second, Malone misread "with his *Tygers hart wrapt in a Players hyde*." By thinking that the line quoted (and altered) was Greene's or one of his friends', Malone ignored, in Alexander's words, "the force which attaches in English to the use of *his* before such a depreciatory quotation: this use of *his* indicates that the victim is being condemned out of his own mouth."[7] Greene in fact provides an example of the sort of rubbish, in his judgment, that Shakespeare writes and we are expected to condemn; and he deliberately misquotes it to get in another hit at the rival's profession as player.

Third, *factotum* did not then mean what it does now: "a man-of-all-work, a servant who does odd jobs about the place" (*OED* Factotum 1.c)—a meaning that might well suggest that Shakespeare, among other tasks, fixed up old plays. It meant, instead, "a person of boundless conceit, who thinks himself able to do anything, however much beyond the reach of real abilities," or, as defined by the *OED*, quoting *Groatsworth*, "a would-be universal genius" (1.a). Such a man would "naturally produce original creations, by which he might display his powers and outshine his rivals." Malone's interpretation had completely reversed the original meaning.[8] Most scholars quickly accepted the Smart-Alexander understanding of the thrust and detail of the attack.

Thus the matter stood until 1951 when John Dover Wilson, in a remarkable essay called "Malone and the Upstart Crow," tried to reestablish Malone.[9] While agreeing with Alexander that the two quartos were memorial reconstructions, Wilson was nonetheless convinced that the *Henry VI* trilogy did contain some work of Greene, Nashe, and perhaps Peele. Malone was therefore right to infer an accusation of literary theft in general and with particular regard to the play from which the line was parodied. Read properly, Greene's allusion allowed for Malone's inference. Greene knew well enough that Shakespeare's work on *Henry VI* was not plagiarism in the modern sense of the term; however, he was angry and desperate, determined to hurt the players if he could, and knew that some readers would accept the accusation without question.

Wilson argued that the "upstart Crow, beautified with our feathers" was Horace's crow, not Aesop's, and was thus in fact a charge of

---

[7] *Shakespeare's "Henry VI" and "Richard III,"* 48.

[8] *Shakespeare: Truth and Tradition*, 168–69.

[9] *Shakespeare Survey* 4 (1951): 56–68. He summarizes his main points in, ed., *Second Part of Henry VI* (Cambridge: University Press, 1952), xiv–xix. Wilson had earlier recorded doubts about the Alexander view in *Essential Shakespeare* (Cambridge: University Press, 1932), 44–49.

plagiarism. In the Aesopian tradition, usually, the crow (or jackdaw) finds or borrows the feathers of one or more birds, and until found out and stripped, proudly represents itself as a better bird. Undeserved pride is the point. The actual source of Greene's image, however, according to Wilson, is Horace's third *Epistle* (I.iii.9–20). There Horace warns a young literary friend, Celsus, against stealing from other writers (in Wilson's translation) "lest those he has robbed should return one day to claim their feathers, when like the crow (*cornicula*) stripped of its stolen splendor (*furtivis nudata coloribus*), he would become a laughing-stock." Moreover, in the same place Horace wonders if Titius, another young writer, "is curbing his muse or letting himself go, to storm and swell in the pompous style of tragic drama"—*An tragica desaevit et ampullatur in arte*. Both the pilferage of Celsus and the bombast of Titius occur together in Shakespeare. Horace's passage was well known, was taken to refer to plagiarism, and indeed Malone had himself recognized it (by quoting "*furtivis coloribus*") as the source for the allusion. Sir John Harington, to give one of Wilson's parallel texts, thought that for its many borrowings his *Metamorphosis of Ajax* (1596) was compared with "*Horace* [*sic*] crow deckt with many fethers."[10] Further, "*Esops* Crow, being pranct with the glorie of others feathers," which Alexander had quoted from Greene's *Francesco's Fortunes*, partook of the Horatian implication. Indeed, Wilson asserted, "Aesop's Crow" was so connected in the Renaissance mind with Horace's as to be "practically identical" with it, since Aesopian collections of the time substitute Horace's "*cornicula*" for the usual "*cornix*" or "*graculus*" (jackdaw) in Aesop.[11]

To support his view Wilson brought forth what appear to be two contemporary reactions to *Groatsworth*. First, Chettle's apology to one of the two who took offense at the letter in the preface to his *Kind-Heart's Dream*:

> With neither of them that take offence was I acquainted, and with one of them [Marlowe] I care not if I never be: The other, whome at that time I did not so much spare, as since I wish I had, for that as I have moderated the heate of living writers, and might have used my owne discretion . . . , because my selfe have seene his demeanor no lesse civill than he exelent in the qualitie

---

[10] *Ulysses upon Ajax* (1596), B1ᵛ.

[11] "Malone and the Upstart Crow," 65. J. A. K. Thomson, in *Shakespeare and the Classics* (London: George Allen & Unwin, 1952), 157–59, thought Greene had the "Latin Aesop" in mind here and in *Francesco's Fortunes*; but the "Latin Aesop" had Horace behind it. If Greene was thinking of vanity, then, "thus applied, the fable loses a good deal of its point."

he professes: Besides, divers of worship have reported, his uprightnes of dealing, which argues his honesty, and his facetious
grace in writting, that aprooves his Art.[12]

Chettle himself has observed Shakespeare's "demeanor" to be as
"civil" as he "exelent in the qualitie he professes" (acting)—thus
answering the charge of pride and, perhaps, the implication ("Anticks") of buffoonery. And others of worth, that is, "several noblemen
interested in defending the slandered poet," have praised his writing—answering the attack on Shakespeare's style (*facetious* meaning
polished and witty).[13]

"But," Wilson asked, "why drag in that pointed reference to
'honesty' and 'uprightnes of dealing'? One does not publicly certify a
friend is no thief unless someone else has previously asserted the
contrary as publicly." The charge had to have been sufficient to
provoke a response at all and clear enough as dishonesty to provoke
this particular one. The specific charge, Wilson noted, is not denied.
Shakespeare just may have been uncomfortable from the sense that,
even if he and his company were well within their rights, "the rewriting of large portions of plays purchased from others was scarcely a
'normal practice.'" In any case, the charge of cruelty, brought home
to the "gentle" Shakespeare by the parallel between the moment
when the dying Richard of York flung into the face of the chief of his
persecutors "O tiger's heart wrapp'd in a woman's hide" (I.iv.137),
words of scorn and hatred, and the pathos of Greene's own death
would have "touched Shakespeare much nearer in September 1592
than any talk of an Upstart Crow."[14]

Wilson's second contemporary testimony was the poem by R. B.,
Gent. (Richard Barnfield?), in *Greene's Funerals*, published in February 1594, but apparently written soon after Greene's death, which
seemed to him, as it has to many, to echo and corroborate the charge
of plagiarism:

> Greene, *is the pleasing Object of an eie:*
> Greene, *pleasde the eies of all that lookt uppon him.*
> Greene, *is the ground of everie Painters die:*
> Greene, *gave the ground, to all that wrote upon him.*

---

[12] Ed. Harrison, 6.
[13] "Malone and the Upstart Crow," 61.
[14] "Malone and the Upstart Crow," 61–62, 64.

Nay more[,] the men, that so Eclipst his fame:
Purloynde his Plumes, can they deny the same?[15]

Wilson has reconverted few to Malone's reading, but he has sent many back to their texts, and the ensuing consideration has not completely cleared the Smart-Alexander reading of doubts Wilson raised. Most of the reaction has sought an accommodation which allows for the Horatian allusion but not for a charge of plagiarism in Wilson's or the modern sense of the word.

Warren B. Austin, basing his case on the whole of *Greene's Funerals*, has argued that R. B. had neither *Groatsworth* nor Shakespeare in mind. R. B. was "merely pointing to a phenomenon his readers would have recognized at once—namely, the wave of exploitation of Greene's name, manner, and style" after his death, in which "all that wrote upon him" would take their cue from his pamphlets because of their enormous success. In the crucial couplet, Austin thinks, R. B. in fact alludes to Gabriel Harvey's effort in his letters, published within days of Greene's death, to blacken (eclipse) Greene's reputation. R. B. therefore was accusing those who, like Harvey, attacked Greene in a style Greene had taught them. "Purloynde his Plumes" repeats against Harvey himself the charge he had made that Greene, in forming his style, had "borrowed and filched plumes." This very image, R. B. saw, was a favorite with Greene.[16]

Austin's argument, while impressive, is not totally convincing. We must believe that Greene was attacked by writers *in addition to* Harvey ("*all* that wrote upon him") *after* his death on the 3rd and *before* Thomas Watson's on the 26th, during which period, Austin takes it, R. B. wrote these poems, attacks "which never reached publication or at least have not come down to us." Unless R. B. was thinking of works *before* Greene's death, *The Defence of Cony-Catching*, for example, or *Groatsworth* and perhaps *Repentance* circulating in some form, and these *not* by Greene himself, then it is hard to understand whom, in addition to Harvey, he had in mind. Austin appears to include the printer Wolfe because Harvey's letters issued from his shop, which is an odd way to think. It is far easier to infer that R. B. had in mind actors who had exploited literary properties that were Greene's and at the same time had darkened his reputation (by spreading rumors)—both, presumably, generally known. But even if R. B. has in mind a

---

[15] Ed. R. B. McKerrow (1911; repr. Stratford-upon-Avon: Shakespeare Head Press, 1922), 81.

[16] "A Supposed Contemporary Allusion to Shakespeare as a Plagiarist," *Shakespeare Quarterly* 6 (1955): 373–80.

kind of plagiarism, the attack in *Groatsworth* need not. "[W]rote upon him" may mean, as E. J. Honigmann suggests, taking *wrote* to mean *wrought*, "worked on the lines laid down by him," in a general sort of dependence, that is, in his love novels or in his plays. To give a second, less likely alternative, perhaps R. B. meant that the basis ("ground") for the account of Greene's dissipation used by *all*, by Harvey and one or both of *Groatsworth* and *Repentance*, available in manuscript or print, was taken from Greene's own (authentic) books of confession and repentance. But *Groatsworth* can be included among the "all" only if R. B. knew it was not authentic. Before Austin, the Smart-Alexander reading took it that R. B. had misread the *Groatsworth* attack as a charge of plagiarism.[17]

Some have questioned Wilson's reading of Chettle's apology. For Janet Spens "his uprightnes of dealing, which argues his honesty" means no more than "his conduct shows him to be a gentleman," with *honesty* meaning *honor* and carrying the connotation of "gentle birth and breeding."[18] For Andrew S. Cairncross the Horatian *honestus* is intended, meaning "decent, gentlemanly," and, in an observation one might well question, "vprightnes of dealing" lacked then the business flavor it has now.[19] As to why Shakespeare and his supporters should so bestir themselves, it is suggested that without including plagiarism the charges are serious enough: ingratitude, desertion, cruelty, and the implication that he is no gentleman. In any case, it has been argued, Chettle's apology, as put, does not require an inference that he was confronted directly for the defense by Shakespeare or anyone.

Johannes fac totum has been taken metaphorically in one reading and quite literally in the other. Alongside the meaning Smart chose, "a would-be universal genius," first in the *OED* (Factotum 1.a), Dover Wilson put "or 'one who meddles with everything' " (1.b), and proceeded to gloss it with such words as "rehandling and revising." *Fac totum*, Smart thought, has "an unlucky ambiguity" about it. We have almost no help from the sixteenth century with the phrase, *Groatsworth*'s use being the first recorded. *Fac totum* was fairly common, both with and without *Magister* or *Dominus*, expanded forms

---

[17] Honigmann, "Shakespeare's 'Lost Source-Plays,' " *Modern Language Review* 49 (1954): 296–97. Austin's view on R. B. has been well received, by S. Schoenbaum, in *Shakespeare's Lives* (New York: Oxford Univ. Press, 1970), 52–53, and Andrew S. Cairncross in his edition of *3 Henry VI* (London: Methuen, 1964), xli–iii.

[18] *TLS*, 15 June 1951, 373; see Wilson's rejoinder on 29 June, 405

[19] Ed., *2 Henry VI* (London: Methuen, 1957), xliii. For his review of Wilson, see *Review of English Studies* 4 (1953): 157–60.

which on occasion were used in contempt or derision, as is the case here. "Jack of all trades," also listed by the *OED* (1.a) where *Groatsworth* is cited, and one preferred by most scholars, has been used with both interpretations. Recorded first in 1618 (*OED*), it seems always to have implied "and master of none," and, at least in one of its forms, "John of all trades," carried the sense "mender" as early as 1637–38. There may be in *Groatsworth*, as I suggest elsewhere, a play on "John Mend-all" or "Amend-all," the names used then by historians and others for the leader of Jack Cade's Revolt. Perhaps the term was inspired by, and thus ridicules Shakespeare through, the Cade episode in *2 Henry VI* that everyone thinks is Shakespeare's and among his first and best.[20]

The main response to Wilson has been the listing of crow-feather images from other passages on actors-writers in order to show either that impudence is the more likely charge or else that Wilson has misinterpreted the nature of the theft suggested by the image and as a consequence has made too much of it. Nashe, in his frequently cited preface to Greene's *Menaphon* (1589), had written of poets who had "tricked up a companie of taffaty fooles [actors] with their feathers," which cannot be taken to imply plagiarism.[21] There have been quotations on Wilson's side as well, two identified by Sidney Thomas before Wilson made his case.[22] Wilson himself added one, from *The Mirror of Modesty*, of 1584, in which Greene apologizes for retelling the story of Susanna found in the Apocrypha:

> But your honor may thinke I play like *Ezops* Crowe, which deckt hir selfe with others feathers, or like the proud Poet *Batyllus*, which subscribed his name to *Virgils* verses, and yet presented them to *Augustus*: In the behalfe therfore of this my offence, I excuse my selfe with the answere that *Varro* made, when he offered *Ennius* workes to the Emperour: I give quoth he another mans picture, but freshlie flourished with mine owne colours.[23]

---

[20] *OED* also gives "*Frère Jean Factotum*" from Paré, at *a.* 1590; cf. McKerrow's notes in, ed., *Nashe*, 4:292, 387–88, which give Erasmus, *Adagia*, 1574, " 'Facere totum,' pro, vim potestatemque omnem habere"; Smart, *Shakespeare: Truth and Tradition*, 168; M. P. Tilley, *Dictionary of Proverbs*, etc. (1950; repr. Ann Arbor: Univ. of Michigan Press, 1966), J19; and my suggestion in *Shakespeare Quarterly* 40 (1989): 491–92. *Jack*, for which *Johannes* is (pretentious) Latin, was a term for a servant, one proverbially no gentleman (Tilley, J3).

[21] Ed. McKerrow, 3:323–24.

[22] "The Meaning of Greene's Attack on Shakespeare," *Modern Language Notes* 66 (1951): 483–84.

[23] *Works*, ed. Grosart, 3:7–8.

Here, for Wilson, it is Horace's thief, not Aesop's mimic, that Greene has in mind, and the question is not the theft of a line or two but the rewriting of a whole literary work. Even Alexander, though he questioned Wilson's interpretation of the *Mirror* passage and continued to defend his own reading, admitted that "Greene's manner of expressing himself is not without a certain ambiguity or confusion, and what may have been obvious at sight to his fellow playwrights is still puzzling to the modern reader," so that the letter taken by itself does not enable us to determine what exactly is meant.[24] The two crows may indeed have merged in the minds of many. But there certainly was a crow distinctive for its pride and not pilferage in much of the Aesop of the day and in many allusions by Greene and others having to do with acting-writing, and this one at least *appears* to be the crow in the attack. Writing in 1970, "after the dust and feathers have settled," S. Schoenbaum has no doubt but that "Alexander has carried the day."[25]

Some who accept that theft is the charge restrict the sense in which such was applicable to Shakespeare. For Honigmann, who lists passages on the conflict between playwrights and actors, "Greene's crow was not meant to suggest that Shakespeare had revised plays by one or two other writers, but that he had pilfered *sententiae* and examples," selected feathers, that is, not the whole cloak.[26] The crow refers, in Cairncross' view, to Shakespeare's "faculty for picking up words and phrases here and there."[27] Such surely was what Nashe intended by "plumes" in his 1589 preface when he complains of "the Italionate penne that, of a packet of pilfries . . . in disguised array, vaunts *Ovids* and *Plutarchs* plumes as theyr owne."[28] Shakespeare absorbed hundreds of such phrases and echoes from a variety

---

[24] *Introductions to Shakespeare* (New York: Norton 1964), 124–27.

[25] *Shakespeare's Lives*, 704. Later, in *William Shakespeare: A Documentary Life* (1975), 116–17, he allows for the possiblity that Greene conflated the two crows and thereby made a double accusation. The crow is Aesop's, according to Baldwin, if one considers the "total genesis of the crow figure," which he tries to do (*Literary Genetics*, 48–49). For other crow images see, H. P. Smith, *Modern Philology* 25 (1927): 83–86; Roy Walker, *TLS*, 10 August 1951, 501; Arthur Freeman, *Notes and Queries* 213 (1968): 129–30; Peter Berek, *Shakespeare Quarterly* 35 (1984): 205–7; note also Greene, 4:103, 12:24, 37; *A Knack To Know a Knave*, lines 1079–80 (ed. Proudfoot [1963]); *James the Fourth*, V.ii.10–11 (ed. Sanders); Chettle's *Piers Plainness*, ed. Winny, 151; *Defence of Conny-Catching*, ed. Harrison, 35. Many find, as H. C. Hart did (ed., *2 Henry VI* [1909, rev. 1931], xiii), "something grotesque" about one of the greatest plagiarists of the day "daring to accuse another writer of plagiarism."

[26] "Shakespeare's 'Lost Source-Plays,' " 295.

[27] Ed., *2 Henry VI*, xliv.

[28] Ed. McKerrow, 3:312.

of sources, including the plays of others. All playwrights did. Just possibly, we may add, this practice is made the basis for a hint at a larger kind of indebtedness. The attack can only hint, if indeed it does, since the basis is so insubstantial. But the charge is expected to assume the weight and legitimacy of those which, having a firmer basis, accompany it: Marlowe's atheism and the actors' ingratitude and pride. There is no indication of the real cause of Shakespeare's ascendancy. It strikes out wildly in several directions at once, from anger and pain, hoping to hurt in return. The passage is now read more as an index to a state of mind, Greene's, than as a clue to Shakespeare's moral sensibility or early methods.

The charge against Shakespeare ought to be seen as part of an ongoing conflict: first, between the University Wits (Greene, Nashe, Peele, and others) and actors, and second, between the Wits and the new, uneducated professional playwrights (Shakespeare, Munday, Kyd, and others). This letter, for Tucker Brooke, "expresses a manly denunciation of one of the cruelest injustices of Elizabethan life: the heart-breaking and pauperizing subservience of the dramatic poets to the managers of theatrical companies."[29] The Wits, in order to survive, had humiliated themselves by writing plays, and as a consequence had given new quality to the popular repertory, had filled the playhouses, and had seen the players grow rich while they themselves were in constant economic distress. They objected, as Alfred Harbage noticed, "simultaneously to the prostitution of their muses and to the low rates paid for prostitution."[30] Moreover, they were now forsaken (Greene) or apt to be (his friends) by the players in favor of non-university trained writers who understood nothing of art and could only imitate their betters (using blank verse, for example) or else steal from them, or something of both.

Nashe's preface to *Menaphon* had described the Wits' services to the common players and established the line and language in the attack we quoted above (page 24): "Sundry other sweete Gentle-

---

[29] *Authorship of the Second and Third Parts*, 191. See Alfred Harbage, *Shakespeare and the Rival Tradition* (1952), chap. 4; Honigmann, "Shakespeare's 'Lost Source-Plays,'" 294–95; Alexander, *Shakespeare's Life and Art* (1929; rev. New York: New York Univ. Press, 1961), 124–26; Baldwin, *Literary Genetics*, chap. 7. Honigmann has argued that Greene's was "a more wide-ranging and more venomously personal attack than has been recognized"; far from being always "gentle," Shakespeare must have been, like Henslowe, a theatrical banker or paymaster, shrewd and sometimes harsh (*Shakespeare's Impact on His Contemporaries* [London: Macmillan, 1982], 1–6).

[30] *Shakespeare and the Rival Tradition*, 95.

men," etc.[31] This passage and attitude, as we have said, must be the source for the account in the narrative portion of *Groatsworth* of the career of the celebrated player-patron who introduces Roberto to playmaking (see Appendix D). To this one player, in Baldwin's judgment, *Groatsworth* "transfers all of Nashe's satiric portrait."[32] Greene had rendered Nashe's passage into narrative through Francesco's experience with the players in *Francesco's Fortunes* in 1590, had given an unkind account of actors in *The Royal Exchange* of the same year, and in *A Quip* of the summer of 1592 had described players as "lowlie," "base-minded," "peacockes and painted asses ... [who] care not howe they get crownes," one of whom "is in his owne imagination, too full of selfe liking and selfe love."[33]

By "Puppets" and "Anticks," then, following Nashe, the attack suggests what the players and plays were like *before* the advent of the Wits and what but for the Wits they still would be. Two quotations, one from Samuel Rowlands in 1600 and the other from *The Return of Parnassus* (Second Part) in about 1601, show how commonplace became the sentiment and expression which was Nashe's and then *Groatsworth*'s:

> Will you stand spending your inventions treasure,
> To teach Stage parrats speake for pennie pleasure,
> While you your selves like musicke-sounding Lutes
> Fretted and strunge, gaine them their silken sutes.

> [Studioso] Better it is mongst fidlers to be chiefe,
> Then at [a] plaiers trencher beg reliefe.
> But ist not strange these mimick apes should prize
> Unhappy Schollers at a hireling rate? ...
> *England* affordes those glorious vagabonds,
> That carried earst their fardels on their backes,
> Coursers to ride on through the gazing streets,
> Sooping it in their glaring Satten sutes ... :
> With mouthing words that better wits have framed
> They purchase lands, and now Esquiers are namde.[34]

---

[31] Ed. McKerrow, 3:323–24.

[32] *Literary Genetics*, 42.

[33] (Gainesville: Scholars' Facs., 1954), H2ʳ.

[34] *Letting of Humours Blood in the Head-Vaine*, A3ʳ; V.i, lines 1916–28; *Three Parnassus Plays (1598–1601)*, ed. J. B. Leishman (London: Nicholson & Watson, 1949), 350. Cf. also John Donne, Sat. II, lines 13–14 (ed. Milgate [1967]): [of one who] "gives ideot actors meanes / (Starving himselfe) to live by'his labor'd sceanes," which may be based on *Groatsworth*; John Davies, *Microcosmos* (1603,

The sneering allusion to Shakespeare's blank verse belongs to a larger context. Apparently himself ridiculed for not being able to write in Marlowe's style, Greene, as early as 1588, in *Perimedes*, derided those "bred of *Merlins* [Marlowe's] race ... that set the end of scollarisme in an English blanck verse."[35] Nashe, in 1589, had followed Greene with an attack on the "ideot Art-masters ... who (mounted on the stage of arrogance) thinke to out-brave better pennes with the swelling bumbast of a bragging blanke verse." Marlowe's imitators, Nashe goes on, the unlearned "triviall translators," probably Kyd, possibly Shakespeare or Munday, some or all, are men without art who derive "many good sentences" from Seneca and can "bodge up a blanke verse with ifs and ands."[36] To this line of argument *Groatsworth*'s slur against Shakespeare is the culmination: this common player is an ignorant, egotistical imitator of a bad style, a specimen of which is given. The general thrust of attack, when one considers this matrix, would appear to be otherwise than against plagiarism as such.

M. C. Bradbrook has directed attention to a theatrical background which helps us see how insulting and cruel the pictorial imagery of the attack was. *Antics*, the "lowest and most scurrilous" form of actors, were grotesquely costumed and painted hybrids of man and beast who performed what were originally speechless parts in low entertainments of wild dance and pointed abuse. A play called *Aesop's Crow*, presented during Edward VI's reign, may have first given speaking parts to these hybrids and may be recalled in the passage. In *Groatsworth*, one of these antics, the crow, not only has learned how to speak but also, spurning his teachers and thereby betraying his true nature as a tiger, has taken to writing. "The kind of player Greene suggests is one who began as a tattered, gaudily dressed stroller, with the slipperiness, the capacity for betrayal, of all wandering tribes—gipsies, fiddlers, minstrels, tinkers."[37]

We cannot know whether some specific injustice, real or imagined, something said or done, directed Greene's wrath against Shakespeare, or did so in such a way, again to speculate, that Chettle knew about

---

Works, ed. Grosart [repr. 1967], 2:82), 214–15, on the wealth and pride of actors: "Onely because (forsooth) they use their *Tongue*, / To speake as they are taught, or right or *wronge*"; and the material on the actors in *Ratsey's Ghost* (1605), B1ᵛ, Rylands facs. (Manchester: Manchester Univ. Press, 1932), how, when they grow rich, they need "care for no man, nor for them that before made thee prowd, with speaking their words upon the Stage."

[35] *Works*, ed. Grosart, 7:8.

[36] Ed. McKerrow, 3:311, 315–16.

[37] "Beasts and Gods: Greene's *Groats-Worth of Witte* and the Social Purpose of *Venus and Adonis*," *Shakespeare Survey* 15 (1962): 62–72, esp. 64.

it. Greene was accused in print in April 1592 of having sold *Orlando Furioso* to both Queen's and Admiral's Men, and of having excused himself on the ground that "there was no more faith to be held with Plaiers, than with them that valued faith at the price of a feather, . . . [for they were] men that measured honestie by profite, and that regarded their Authors not by desart, but by necessitie of time."[38] Dover Wilson thought that Shakespeare may have had something to do with the "boycott which almost certainly followed."[39] The "Arch-plaimaking-poet" Roberto in the *Groatsworth* narrative likewise "slightly [meaning *sleightly?*] dealt with them that did him good," that is, the players; when "paid anything afore-hand," he broke his promise (lines 715–22). Whatever the case, the players apparently had done with Greene, which he knew in the late summer of 1592, and he was thus deprived of a major source of income. They had Shakespeare, one of their own, who was prolific, popular, and no trouble.

We have looked with slight success in Shakespeare's works for signs of this early disturbance. Bradbrook thinks *Venus and Adonis*, published in April 1593, "a counter challenge of nobility by a common player."[40] The same could be said of *Midsummer Night's Dream*, usually assigned to the plague years, with its Ovidian sophistication and cultured audience. Many, following Charles Knight in 1840, find an allusion to Greene in the work listed by Philostrate: "The thrice three Muses mourning for the death / Of learning, late deceas'd in beggary." "Some satire, keen and critical," Theseus decides, inappropriate for a nuptial (V.i.52–54). In Dover Wilson's view Shakespeare here replies to the urgings of friends that he respond in kind to Greene. Such "would be easy to write," Shakespeare implies, "but—the man is dead, and so enough."[41] The word *o'er-green*, an apparent coinage, in Sonnet 112 in a complaint about a "vulgar scandal" has led some to detect an allusion:

> Your love and pity doth th'impression fill
> Which vulgar scandal stamp'd upon my brow;
> For what care I who calls me well or ill
> So you o'ergreen my bad, my good allow?

We may also suspect a clue to Shakespeare's reaction in Polonius'

---

[38] *Defence of Conny-Catching*, ent. S. R. 21 April 1592, ed. G. B. Harrison (1924; repr. New York: Barnes & Noble, 1966), 37.

[39] "Malone and the Upstart Crow," 65.

[40] "Beast and Gods," 63.

[41] Ed., *Midsummer Night's Dream* (Cambridge: University Press, 1940), 93–94.

response to Hamlet's "the most beautified Ophelia"; "That's an ill phrase, a vile phrase, 'beautified' is a vile phrase" (II.ii.110–12). And some have found in Falstaff's death, rejected and pathetic, he of the "green fields," something of Greene's death.[42] Shakespeare worked that way, touching lightly upon the local and familiar. Almost twenty years later, when he turned to Greene's *Pandosto* for the plot of *Winter's Tale*, his play of jealousy and reconciliation, he had made peace with the ghost of Greene. As for the ghost, we had best not speculate, since Shakespeare took "more verbal echoes from *Pandosto*" than from any other novel he used as a source (Kenneth Muir).[43]

---

[42] Baldwin Maxwell gives the case tongue-in-cheek, in "The Original of Sir John Falstaff—Believe It or Not," *Studies in Philology* 27 (1930): 230–32.

[43] *Shakespeare's Sources: I. Comedies and Tragedies* (London: Methuen, 1957), 247. Baldwin wondered if "Is it not strange" alludes to *Strange*'s company (*Literary Genetics*, 47). He thought "seeke you better Maisters" means "write for some other company than the *combined* company." We might also hear in "those burres" the *Burbages*.

Appendix H

"the waspish little worme"

As the end approached, "Greene," like Socrates awaiting execution, undertook to versify Aesop. The fable of the ant and grasshopper, which comes just before the end (lines 985–1044), is in situation and moral the traditional version of the imprudent grasshopper who, having sung the summer away while the careful ant labored, dies of starvation, his pleas for succor unanswered. Though Aesop had been a fixture in the schools time out of mind, this appears to be the first version in print in English verse (though there are poetic allusions to the motif), the first to mix prose and verse, and the longest and most elaborate treatment of the fable up to this time. Its most distinctive feature, however, the source of its power and complexity, derives from the fact that it identifies Greene personally and absolutely with the grasshopper—"Like him my selfe: like me. . . ." Greene wasted his youthful vigor and now, unprovided, dies from weakness, serving as a lesson to all youth. In consequence a good deal of the energy in the fable is directed not, with the manifest moral, against Greene, but rather against others. The ant and the others of his one-time friends, who may include the ant ("his olde acquaintance"), have let him down—*they* are responsible—so that the old fable gets a little out of shape in order to serve as a pretext for an attack on them. It seems to catch, in statement and counterstatement, a special balance of anger at others and self reproach. It is one fragment we might want, given the intensity of its inner conflict, to think Chettle got from Greene.

For E. A. J. Honigmann, it continues "in a new context that is more insidiously damaging" the charges against the theatrical establishment already expressed in the celebrated letter and—a conclusion "it becomes difficult to resist"—Shakespeare *is* the ant.[1] This is the

---

[1] *Shakespeare's Impact*, 1–6; anticipated by Alden Brooks, *Will Shakspere: Factotum and Agent* (1937), 83–84; *Will Shakspere and the Dyer's Hand* (1943), 36. I quote from Honigmann. Russell Fraser, for one, accepts an allusion to Shakespeare, in *Young Shakespeare*, 142.

Shakespeare, Honigmann argues, who emerged in the period 1590–94 as a theatrical banker or paymaster, another Philip Henslowe, grown rich, partly, Greene would have felt, at his expense, and now, in Greene's need, refuses assistance. The language of the grasshopper's reproof of the ant, in its severity, which is without precedent in the Aesopic tradition, does indeed sound personal and may suggest the earlier accusations against "Shake-scene":

> *The greedy miser thirsteth still·for gaine,*
> *His thrift is theft, his weale works others woe....*

Here are theft, injury to others (that is, according to Honigmann, putting other playwrights out of business), and cruelty. Greene "manages to make thrift seem thoroughly inhuman—indeed, repulsive." Here, too, are the warnings he gave against misplaced trust: (1) "Yes trust them not: for there is an upstart Crow"; (2) "Trust not then ... to such weake staies"; (3) *"Trust to thy selfe, small hope in want yeeld friends"*; (4) "like me, shall all that trust to friends...." Beast fables, it is true, were expected to say something else, something specific and real—the case, as we have seen, with *"Lamilias Fable."* We are expected to see that Greene is talking about himself; *Greene* occurs three times. (Greene himself might have felt no need to insist on what would be obvious.) In his fourth letter, dated 11 and 12 September, just over a week after Greene's death, Harvey has a passage which makes the same connection and may suggest that it was common: "Alas, he is pitifully bestead, that ... is constrained to make woeful *Greene,* and beggarly *Pierce Pennylesse,* (as it were a Grashopper, and a Cricket, two pretty musitians, but silly creatures) the argumente of his stile ...: howsoever the Grashopper enraged, would bee no lesse then a greene Dragon...."[2]

Honigmann is certainly justified in tracing the anger here to the theatrical establishment, but the equation of the ant with Shakespeare can only be a good possibility. A moneylender other than Henslowe or Shakespeare may have been affiliated with Burbage. Honigmann's case takes on some strength from what may be code in the verbal texture of the fable, something more than the *ant* = *antic* possibility (recall the "Anticks" = actors of the letter), especially since so much is made over the name *Greene.* We notice *weale* ("*his* weale *works others* woe"), one *will* ("*as wantons* will"), another ("*which* will *in caves remain"*), another ("*I* will *relentless rest"*), and still another ("*toyes that* will *deceive"*). More conspicuous is the word *spares* ("*thriftie husband*

---

[2] *Foure Letters,* ed. Harrison, 72.

spares") which might well matter, though it is an obvious translation of the *parcet* (or other forms of *parceo*) frequent in Latin versions of the fable.[3] Spenser has Cuddie in the October Eclogue, just before a two-line allusion to the fable, regret that his "poore Muse hath spent her spared store" (line 9). The moral in William Bullokar's 1585 version is "he that spareth not shall at length beg."[4] The wordplay possible here does occur, in my judgment, in Shakespeare's epitaph: "BLEST BE THE MAN THAT SPARES THES STONES." Still, we wish these potential clues were highlighted in some more suggestive way (a dying Greene might not feel obliged to be secretive), that a case so intriguing were a little stronger. The ant will have to do, simply, as the type of prudent, former friend.

Curiously, the poem passes up the chance to sharpen the taunt of the ant with the retort present in full half the extant versions—"*Si aestate contasti, hieme salta*"—and to intensify sympathy for the grasshopper with a defense he is frequently permitted—"*Non michi vacabant: per sepes oberrabam cantando,*" and "*Ego tunc illis qui laborabant cecini, et nichil mercedis ab eis recepi.*"[5] We might wish, too, that the poet had availed himself, less indirectly, of the great, primarily Greek tradition in which the grasshopper is among the highest symbols of civilization, before, in Don Cameron Allen's words, he "leaves the myrtles and laurels of the Greek sea islands to inhabit for a while the north of cold and sunlessness."[6] In antiquity the grasshopper was beloved of the muses, symbol of the poet singer, an aristocrat, and badge of royalty. Nonetheless, *Groatsworth*'s humble, pained version, with its grasshopper who finds no value in his life, who knows he

---

[3] See, e.g., the prose version of Avianus by William Harmanns (Guielmo Hermano) in Martin Dorp's *Fabularum* (1515), E1ʳ: "*et qui non parcuit, olim mendicabit.*" For Latin versions of the fable by and based on Phaedrus and Avianus, and by others, see Leopold Hervieux, *Les Fabulistes Latins*, 5 vols., 2d edn. (first two vols., Paris: Librairie de Firmin-Didot, 1884, other vols., 1893–99; repr. New York: B. Franklin, 1964), 2:227–28, 245, 473, 558, 724, 772, 802–3, 3:283, 366–67, 397–98, 446, 473, 499, 4:435. The Greek of Babrius is #140 in Ben E. Perry's *Babrius and Phaedrus* (Cambridge, MA: Harvard Univ. Press, 1965). English versions are by Caxton (1484) and his successors (1550?, 1560?, 1570?), Alexander Barclay's version of Mantuan's (comp. 1514, pr. 1570), George Turberville's version of the same (1567), Geoffrey Whitney (1586), William Bullokar (1585, STC 187), Francis Eglesfield (1651), and James Shirley (1656).

[4] STC 187, 69.

[5] In Hervieux, ed., 2:227–28, 245, 558.

[6] *Image and Meaning: Metaphoric Traditions in Renaissance Poetry* (Baltimore: The Johns Hopkins Press, 1960), 88. Allen gives numerous references to the non-Aesopian tradition.

deserves better than he gets, ought to have a place alongside its more illustrious progeny in English, the grasshopper poems of Lovelace, Cowley, Keats, and Hunt.

Glossary

ability-ie] means (in general).

abject] outcast.

admired] wonderful, surprising.

advizde] knowing, judicious.

amated] astonished, overwhelmed.

amisse] error (*euph.* for evil way).

Angels] gold coins (worth about ten shillings).

Arch-plaimaking-poet] i.e., chief or best (with contempt, a nonce expression).

assurance] security.

Beldam] loathsome old woman, a hag.

bite his lip] i.e., out of suppressed anger.

Brothell] abandoned woman, prostitute (*OED*).

capping and reverence] obeisance (made by removing the cap and bowing).

carelesnes] neglect.

carelesse] unconcerned.

casseerd] dismissed from service (cashiered).

checkt him] stopped him suddenly.

childes right] birthright (inheritance due as firstborn).

compassed] obtained (through trickery).

con you little thanke] offer you slight thanks.

conceipt] *sb.* (1) capacity to understand, (2) fanciful idea(s) or expression(s), (3) conception, imagination; *v.* apprehend, imagine.

conceited] fanciful.

Consilium post facta] "Wisdom after the event."

conge] bow.

consort of musike] company of musicians.

consorts] *sb.* companions; *v.* joins.

conversation (line 143)] behavior, mode of life.

conversing with] (1) keeping company with, (2) having sex with.

copesmate] partner in mischief.

courses] ways, undertakings (*OED* 21.b, citing line 945 first).

course] way of life.

court like] with great courtesy.
crancke] lusty, "cocky"(?) (*OED a.*1).
cranker] more aggressively high-spirited, "cockier."
credit] (favorable) reputation (1) in general, (2) for solvency.
croucht] cringed submissively.
Crownes] coins (worth five shillings).
curiously] fastidiously.
Emmets] ant's. Chiefly *dial.*, sometimes *poet.* or *arch.* (*OED*).
entertainement] (1) (line 323) welcome (of a guest), (2) (line 330) provision for reception.
entire affect] sincere affection.
equall] just, impartial (Lat. *aequus*).
exercise] employment.
faine] lie.
fall unto] begin (*fall to*) food.
fetch their compasse] take their roundabout course.
fingerd] got hold of (implying through false means).
fonde] foolish.
foole-holy] foolishly virtuous (only cit. in *OED*).
forward] ardent, eager.
frowardnes] perversity.
furnish this pageant] accomplish or complete this scene (ruse).
goe] walk.
gracer] one who graces or gives grace to (*OED*, citing line 888 first).
gratious] attractive, pleasing.
Gray] badger, probably (*OED* Grey *sb.*6), an *obs.* sense.
hardly] cannot easily, only with difficulty (*OED* 6)?
hazard] game of dice (our "craps"?).
husband] manager (of affairs or business).
in like sort] in the same manner (i.e., with a warning).
in her eare] in a whisper, privately.
indirect] not fair and open, not honest.
intertainment (line 319)] welcome, reception (welcoming speech?).
invective] abusive (satirical).
just (line 777)] (1) exact, (2) deserved (?).
justified] affirmed.
keepe forme] i.e., good order.
knit up] tie together, compress.
large] i.e., (ironically) relaxed, easy.
leveld against] aimed at.
levell] aim.
licentious] immoral.
lightly] clearly (unquestionably).

light] fig., mental illumination or elucidation (*OED* 6).

make one] join in the company (*OED* Make 26).

make no doubt] raise no question (implying a question could be raised).

make-shifte] shifty, roguish (*OED*'s only listing as adj.).

meane] intend.

meaninge] intention.

meant (line 388)] intended.

meat] food (in general).

meere] nothing short of, downright.

mislike] am displeased with or offended at.

mockt] deceived.

momentanie] momentary.

Multa cadunt inter calicem supremaque labra] "There's many a slip between the cup and the lip."

negligent] i.e., idle, slothful.

next] nearest.

O horrenda fames] "Oh dreadful poverty!"

O mors quam amara] "Oh death how bitter."

one selfe] one and the same.

ornaments] i.e., attire or something worn purely to adorn.

outcountenanst] embarrassed, with the suggestion of bluffed.

passing at] surpassing at, pre-eminent in.

passion] passionate speech.

plaine] smooth; or, perhaps, simple.

practise] plot.

prevent] (1) frustrate, bring to nought, (2) avoid.

prompter (line 339)] i.e., "one who helps a speaker" (*OED* 2, citing this first).

proper] (1) true, (2) own.

proves] establishes as true (presents the case for).

recken with] settle accounts with.

recurelesly] incurably (only instance in *OED*).

report] reputation.

rest] remain.

rested in] (1) occupied (*OED* 3); (2), perhaps, trusted in or relied on (ironically, 6).

Ruffler] proud swaggering fellow.

salve her credit] preserve her good name (antedates *OED* v.[2] 4).

serched] penetrated.

shadowing] concealing.

simperd it] smiled in a silly, self-conscious or affected manner (*OED* v.1.b).

skilles not] matters not.

smoothing] flattering.

snuffe] portion of the wick (of a candle or oil lamp).

sodenly] immediately.

solempnitie] festive celebration (often nuptial).

sonnet] any short lyric, especially a love song.

sooth] flatter.

soothed] encouraged.

spares] saves (*OED* 5.b).

specialties] "special contract[s], obligation[s], or bond[s], expressed in
   an instrument under seal" (*OED*).

spoiled] (1) destroyed, (2) plundered, robbed.

stale] decoy.

stay-staies] prop(s), support(s).

subject] recipient (*OED* 12).

Tables] i.e., backgammon.

tearms of] addresses of, or (language in general) appropriate to.

trained] (1) traced or tracked (*OED*, citing line 421 first), (2) enticed.

trickly] (1) finely, (2) cleverly, in an effort to deceive.

trickt himselfe up] "decked himself out."

Tu tibi cura] "Look to thyself."

unequally (line 127)] With a suggestion of *unjustly* (Lat. *aequus*).

unequall] unjust (Lat. *aequus*).

visited] punished.

wantons] those spoiled by over-indulgence.

weale] well-being, prosperity.

wel taken] (1) captured, (2) heard, understood.

werried] seized by the throat with their teeth and torn (*OED* Worry
   1).

wild] willed.

wit] wisdom, prudent knowledge.

woonning] dwelling.

worme] The word could refer to almost any kind of insect (*OED* 2).

wringing] pressing.

writ up] i.e., in her book of accounts owed.

Index

This Index lists proper names in the introduction, in notes to the text, and in the appendices.

Greene's Groatsworth of Wit proclaims itself the death-bed repentance of the Elizabeth poet and playwright Robert Greene. It is the source for the first notice of Shakespeare in London, the celebrated attack on the "Upstart Crow," and alludes to Christopher Marlowe, Thomas Nashe and George Peele, among others. The text is introduced with a full discussion of its peculiar circumstances of publication, its sources, and its date. Carroll produces evidence, some of it new, that Henry Chettle, the printer who admitted editing the book, was probably responsible for much, if not all, of it.

Appendices provide extended discussions of familiar allusions. Of particular interest is the complex history of the interpretation of the "Upstart Crow" passage, as well as a previously unexplicated inflammatory attack against William Cecil, Lord Burghley, in beast fable form, that helps explain the hostile reaction to the book's first edition. The book includes extensive commentary on all difficult or otherwise interesting passages and supplies a full collation of the six early texts and a glossary. This is the first edition based on a comparison of the early texts, and the first with apparatus since A. B. Grosart's at the end of the 19th century.

D. Allen Carroll is professor of English and head of the department at the University of Tennessee in Knoxville. He is the editor of *Skialethia, or A Shadowe of Truth, in Certaine Epigrams and Satyres* by Everard Guilpin (Chapel Hill: University of North Carolina Press, 1974), and he compiled *A Midsummer Night's Dream: An Annotated Bibliography* (New York: Garland, 1986) with Gary Jay Williams. Professor Carroll is also the author of numerous articles, and was the recipient of the University of Tennessee Alumni Outstanding Teaching Award in 1989.